The Euro – the Beginning, the Middle … and the End?

The Euro – the Beginning, the Middle ... and the End?

EDITED BY PHILIP BOOTH

WITH CONTRIBUTIONS FROM

PHILIP BOOTH

FRANCISCO CABRILLO

JUAN E. CASTAÑEDA

JOHN CHOWN

JAMIE DANNHAUSER

KEVIN DOWD

KATJA HENGSTERMANN

BODO HERZOG

ANDREW LILICO

PATRICK MINFORD

NEIL RECORD

PEDRO SCHWARTZ

The Institute of Economic Affairs

First published in Great Britain in 2013 by
The Institute of Economic Affairs
2 Lord North Street
Westminster
London SW1P 3LB
in association with Profile Books Ltd

The mission of the Institute of Economic Affairs is to improve public understanding of
the fundamental institutions of a free society, with particular reference to the role of
markets in solving economic and social problems.

A CIP catalogue record for this book is available from the British Library.

ISBN 978 0 255 36680 9
eISBN 978 0 255 36683 0

Many IEA publications are translated into languages other than English or are reprinted.
Permission to translate or to reprint should be sought from the Director General at the
address above.

Typeset in Stone by MacGuru Ltd
info@macguru.org.uk

Printed and bound in Britain by Hobbs the Printers

CONTENTS

ABOUT THE AUTHORS

Philip Booth

Philip Booth is Editorial and Programme Director of the Institute of Economic Affairs and Professor of Insurance and Risk Management at Cass Business School, City University. He has written extensively on regulation, social insurance and Catholic social teaching. He is a fellow of the Institute of Actuaries and of the Royal Statistical Society and deputy editor of *Economic Affairs*. He has also advised the Bank of England on financial stability issues (1998–2002) and has been a visiting fellow at Blackfriars Hall, Oxford University (2010–11). Philip Booth was also extensively involved in the development of actuarial science and investment and finance education in central and eastern Europe in the post-communist period.

Francisco Cabrillo

Francisco Cabrillo is Professor of Economics at Complutense University, Madrid. A law and economics scholar, Professor Cabrillo has written extensively on regulation, courts, legal origins and economic development and the institutions of the European Union. He is author (with S. Fitzpatrick) of *The Economics of Courts and Litigation* (Edward Elgar, 2008).

Juan E. Castañeda

Juan Castañeda is a Doctor of Economics (2003) and has been a lecturer in economics at the University of Buckingham since 2012. He was a visiting researcher at Cass Business School (2004–05) and a former lecturer at UNED university (1998–2012). He has experience researching in monetary policy and central banking. He is the editor of the blog 'theoldladyofthreadneedlestreet.wordpress.com'.

John Chown

John Chown read economics at Cambridge, winning the Adam Smith Prize for an essay on fixed versus floating exchange rates. He went on to make his career in international tax through his own firm, as a co-founder of the Institute for Fiscal Studies and as a policy adviser to governments on the taxation of currency and capital markets. Tax apart, he wrote *A History of Money* and *A History of Monetary Unions* and is now a regular contributor to *Central Banking*.

Jamie Dannhauser

Jamie Dannhauser joined Lombard Street Research (LSR) in September 2006 after completing his studies at Trinity College, Cambridge, and the Judge Business School, Cambridge. He is currently the senior UK economist at LSR, but also contributes extensively to the firm's coverage of the euro area, developed-world monetary policy and global macroeconomic trends more generally. For much of the crisis, he has been heading up coverage of Europe's periphery economies. Representing the company, Jamie has written articles for the *Wall Street Journal*, the *Financial Times* and *Financial World*. He is a member of the Institute of Economic Affairs' Shadow Monetary Policy Committee.

Kevin Dowd

Kevin Dowd is Professor of Finance and Economics at Durham Business School. He has written extensively on free banking, central banking and bank regulation, monetary economics, financial risk management and pensions. His books include *Private Money: The Path to Monetary Stability* (IEA Hobart Paper 112, recently reissued as an e-publication), *Laissez-Faire Banking* (Routledge, 1992), *Competition and Finance: A Reinterpretation of Financial and Monetary Economics* (Macmillan, 1996) and, most recently (with Martin Hutchinson), *Alchemists of Loss: How Government Finance and Government Intervention Crashed the Financial System* (Wiley, 2010).

Katja Hengstermann

Katja Hengstermann (MBA) was a research assistant at the Institute of Finance and Economics at ESB Business School. She was also a student in International Business (IB) at ESB Business School and Portland State University. Since 2013, Ms Hengstermann has been working as a professional consultant.

Bodo Herzog

Dr Bodo Herzog is Professor of Economics and director of the Institute of Finance and Economics at ESB Business School, Reutlingen University. He was visiting professor at Portland State University, California State University and International University Macedonia, and research fellow at the Massachusetts Institute of Technology (MIT). Professor Herzog's research focuses mainly on macroeconomics and monetary policy, in particular fiscal–monetary interaction in EMU. From 2005 to 2007, Dr Herzog was Chief Economist and Head of the Economics Department at Konrad-Adenauer-Foundation in Berlin and senior economist for the German Council of Economic Experts.

Andrew Lilico

Dr Andrew Lilico is the chairman of Europe Economics, a fellow of the IEA and a member of the Shadow Monetary Policy Committee. He has written extensively on European affairs since the mid-1990s, and has led EU-related projects for the European Commission, European Parliament, FSA, BIS, City of London, Open Europe, major pharmaceuticals firms and others. His team's analysis of the pros and cons of EU-level setting of financial services regulation, on behalf of Open Europe, informed the UK government's (rejected) powers repatriation request at the notorious December 2011 Fiscal Union Treaty negotiations.

Patrick Minford

Patrick Minford is Professor of Applied Economics at Cardiff Business School, Cardiff University. From 1976 to 1997 he was Professor of Applied Economics at Liverpool University. Patrick sat as a member of the Monopolies Commission during the early to mid-1990s and was one of HM Treasury's Panel of Forecasters ('Six Wise Men') from January 1993 to December 1996. He was appointed CBE in 1996.

Neil Record

Neil Record was educated at Balliol College, Oxford, and University College, London. He worked in the 1970s as an economist at the Bank of England, and in 1983 founded Record Currency Management, a specialist institutional currency manager. He has authored *Currency Overlay* (Wiley, 2003), and numerous articles on currency and other areas of risk management, as well as several papers on public sector pensions. He is a frequent speaker at industry conferences and seminars in the UK, the USA and Europe, and in 2012 was a finalist in the Wolfson Economics Prize. He is a Visiting Fellow and Investment Committee member of Nuffield College, Oxford, and a trustee of the Institute of Economic Affairs.

Pedro Schwartz

Dr Pedro Schwartz is Rafael del Pino Research Professor at the Universidad CEU San Pablo in Madrid, after having been professor of economics at three Spanish universities. Previously he was a member of the Research Department of the Bank of Spain. From 2006 to 2008 he was an expert at the Economic and Monetary Committee of the European Parliament. He published *The Euro as Politics* for the IEA (2004).

FOREWORD

Even the most enthusiastic supporters of the creation of a single European currency surely have to confess that things have not turned out as they had hoped, nor as they had expected. In 1998, the then leader of the British Conservative Party, William Hague, warned that membership of the euro could amount to being in a burning building with no exits. A recurring theme of the various arguments in this monograph is whether or not the building was always going to be engulfed by fire and whether political considerations, rather than economic reasoning, have been responsible for closing off the possible exits. Can the fire be extinguished, can fire escapes still be constructed or does the entire building need to be condemned and something wholly different established in its place?

But if supporters of the euro zone have seen their dreams dashed, it remains the case – at least at the time of writing – that those forecasting the single currency's demise have underestimated the euro's resilience, even if such resilience has been largely based on the substantial reservoirs of political will to preserve and sustain the 'project'.

This publication seeks to shift the debate about the euro towards rational economic thinking. It emphatically does not provide a forecast about exactly what will happen and when, nor does it put forward a single blueprint as a solution to the currency's woes. Instead, it provides a wide range of differing analyses and proposals, all from a pro-market perspective. It will therefore be impossible for the reader to agree with everything within these covers – although, unsurprisingly, all the contributors advocate a departure from the prevailing status quo.

If, as many are predicting at the start of 2013, the prospect of a catastrophic, imminent and disorderly break-up of the euro has receded for the time being, it can only be hoped that this will provide the intellectual space for a debate about the management and construction of the single currency and the changes needed over the longer term. The day-to-day crisis management which has catapulted the euro's troubles into the media spotlight might now be replaced by a more measured discussion about reform, amendment or even abolition of the euro. This monograph represents a serious and weighty contribution to that debate, and the authors – as is typical of IEA publications – make proposals that are more imaginative than any that are currently being discussed in the political arena.

For decades, the Institute of Economic Affairs has produced peer-reviewed papers challenging the prevailing economic orthodoxy and positing market-oriented alternatives. It has often taken many years of educational engagement before these free market ideas have entered the intellectual mainstream. But, with this publication, perhaps the Institute has a head start. Fewer and fewer people can now credibly claim that the status quo is optimal or desirable as far as the single currency is concerned. This monograph constitutes a comprehensive and impressive contribution to one of the most controversial and complex economic issues of our times. If there is already an appetite for change, one can only hope that the proposals and analyses in this volume are carefully considered, intelligently discussed and – in some cases – perhaps actually enacted, sooner rather than later.

MARK LITTLEWOOD

Director General and Ralph Harris Fellow,

Institute of Economic Affairs

February 2013

The views expressed in this monograph are, as in all IEA publications, those of the author and not those of the Institute (which has no corporate view), its managing trustees, Academic Advisory Council members or senior staff. With some exceptions, such as with the publication of lectures, all IEA monographs are blind peer-reviewed by at least two academics or researchers who are experts in the field.

SUMMARY

- The UK decided not to join the euro on economic grounds. This was a decision which met with approval from the vast majority of UK liberal economists and which has been proved right by the course of events. Indeed, even the major supposed benefit of the euro – reduced currency volatility – is questionable when the volatility of sterling and the euro against other world currencies is considered.
- The euro zone – even without the UK – was not an optimal currency area. Many proponents of the euro thought that it would evolve into an optimal currency area through structural reform and economic convergence. This has not happened in practice.
- Differences in financial systems between euro zone members meant that their economies responded very differently to global economic shocks and to the ECB's monetary policy operations. This helped to create the financial imbalances that became unsustainable.
- With the possible exception of Ireland, product and labour markets in euro zone members are too rigid to respond adequately to economic shocks. The result has been high unemployment and low or negative economic growth in a number of euro zone countries.
- In general, floating exchange rates are likely to deal with economic shocks at lower cost than fixed exchange rates or single currency arrangements. This was not the major consideration, however, when countries decided to join the euro. Many of the countries that joined the single currency did so because it was thought that external discipline on domestic governments would have beneficial long-term effects.
- Historical evidence suggests that monetary unions that have not

been followed by political unions have tended to fail. This does not mean that such unions are impossible. In this respect, however, the euro was an experiment. It might be possible to proceed from the current position to a euro zone made up of a smaller number of countries. Any countries participating in a single currency should, however, examine carefully their long-term fiscal balance sheets if the strong are not to become responsible for the debts of the weak. This process should include careful analysis of pension and other long-term liabilities. Indeed, if the euro survives the current crisis, it could be brought down by government indebtedness caused by pension liabilities.

- It is very difficult for countries to leave the euro although members could be suspended. Suspension should happen in the case of Greece, at least. This could be followed by the adoption of parallel currency systems whereby the euro can be used alongside new domestic currencies in those member states that are suspended. Currency competition would complement a more general agenda for decentralisation in the EU.

- If there is a break-up of the euro, it is extremely important that it happens in an orderly way. This will be difficult to achieve because the EU elite are unwilling to countenance the possibility that the euro might break up and will therefore not plan for such an eventuality. A break-up of the euro must go hand in hand with vigorous promotion of free trade in the difficult political environment that will exist.

- An alternative solution to the euro crisis would be to return the euro to its founding principles. There could be very strict enforceable *ex ante* rules that all member countries had to meet. Countries that did not abide by the rules would take no part in the economic and monetary policy decisions of the EU or would be suspended from membership.

- EU states could also decide that monetary policy should be decoupled from government altogether. The euro has not succeeded as a single currency with its current institutional mechanisms, and state currencies have often proved to be inflationary. On the other hand, free banking systems create the right incentives for bankers to act prudently and to not inflate the money supply.

TABLES AND FIGURES

The Euro – the Beginning, the Middle … and the End?

1 INTRODUCTION

Philip Booth

The euro: the beginning, the middle and ... the end?

Economists and politicians make so many predictions that it can be diffi-cult to keep track of who has been right and who has been wrong in the great debates of our time. Occasionally, economists and politicians are brave enough to admit that they called a particular decision wrongly and are able to explain why. But, by and large, they continue with their repu-tations intact, regardless of whether they were right or wrong.

This is partly because the nature of economics is such that there is never a perfect controlled experiment. Those who are apparently wrong when making a prediction can always claim that some additional variable affected the outcome in ways that were not taken into account in their model or that things would have been worse if another course of action had been taken.

In this context, it is interesting that economists who broadly support a market economy were on opposite sides of the euro debate at the end of the twentieth century. In general, UK supporters of a market economy opposed the euro and continental supporters of a market economy supported the euro. In 1999, Professor Otmar Issing, giving the IEA Hayek lecture, said: 'I am convinced that the Euro 11 governments have, in principle, taken the correct route to monetary union' (Issing, 2000: 36). On the other hand, Patrick Minford, also writing for the IEA, stated in 2002: 'The final conclusion must be that it is strongly against the British interests to join EMU as it is constituted and planned' (Minford, 2002: 57).

With this in mind, this monograph begins by examining the start of the euro project. The early chapters ask whether, from the economic perspective, it was ever likely to succeed both from the perspective of the UK and from that of other EU countries.

At the time of writing we are in the middle of a crisis. That crisis is being continually postponed by the European Central Bank (ECB) but the crisis has not gone away. The middle chapters examine the nature of that crisis and whether there is any way to either break up the euro without chaos or develop other imaginative solutions that would, temporarily or permanently, resolve the euro zone's problems.

The question on the minds of many observers is whether the euro crisis will – or should – mark the end of the euro as a single currency covering the majority of EU nations. As at the beginning of the project, free market economists are split on this issue, and this is reflected in our authors' proposals. One author identifies what might be termed the 'Charge of the Light Brigade problem'. It could be argued that the euro was correct in its inception – in other words that Issing was right (at least as far as continental countries were concerned). The execution was mishandled, however, in that the necessary liberalisation of markets did not happen and countries have become implicitly responsible for each other's debts. The euro has a bad reputation and has not worked out well but, really, it is the 'commanders' who have been at fault. This perspective suggests that reform is necessary to ensure that the no-bail-out principle is hardwired into the euro system. A second perspective argues for the return to national currencies and two other authors argue for a free banking regime and a currency choice regime.

In summary, all the authors argue that we should be at the end of the euro experiment as we have come to know it: radical reform is necessary.

The beginning

For some years before the euro was adopted a number of IEA authors warned about the consequences. Those warnings were dismissed by passionate supporters of the euro, but rarely were the underlying economic arguments effectively challenged. Indeed, even the free market supporters of the euro believed that radical economic change was necessary in order to bring about the flexibility in labour and product markets that would allow the single currency to succeed.

Those opposing the adoption of the euro suggested that imposing a single currency across a diverse economic area would lead to serious problems when economic shocks hit particular parts of the euro zone. There were warnings given about the inevitable drift towards centralisation that would arise as EU institutions tried to resolve the problems caused by the imposition of the single currency. IEA authors were concerned about the inflationary bias that would arise from using a single currency across several countries as the European Central Bank – whatever its remit – would always wish to conduct monetary policy to stave off serious recession in part of the euro zone. Many authors also cited the difficulties of running a currency union without a single sovereign government and the problems that could be created by huge pension liabilities in many euro zone member states.

While these arguments prevailed among British liberal economists, the positions taken were different among liberal economists in continental Europe. They argued that government fiscal policy and debt management had to be entirely separated from the management of the ECB if the euro were to be successful in the long term: this, in turn, would enforce fiscal discipline on member states. Furthermore, it was maintained that the adoption of the euro would force member states to liberalise their economies so that they would not suffer to the same extent from 'sticky' prices and wages following economic shocks. Finally, and following on from that point, liberal continental economists accused their UK counterparts of following Keynesian doctrines of desiring money illusion as a way of dealing with economic shocks rather than subscribing to a sound, independently managed currency. Both these perspectives are represented in this monograph on the euro.

The monograph begins with a chapter by Patrick Minford that demonstrates the dangers that would have been faced had the UK joined the euro. He argues that, unlike in other EU countries, the UK took the decision whether or not to join purely on economic grounds. The proponents of the euro argued that there would be gains from the elimination of currency fluctuations. Minford shows, however, that any reduction in currency fluctuations could have been nullified because fluctuations of the euro against the dollar were greater than fluctuations of sterling against the dollar. Minford also argues that the costs of joining the euro were much greater than those anticipated even by eurosceptics. He ends by discussing the costs of UK involvement in the whole EU project.

These economic arguments that were so important in the UK revolved around the issue of whether the euro zone would have been an optimal currency area with the UK included. Jamie Dannhauser examines whether the euro zone is an optimal currency area even without the UK. Surely, the theory of optimal currency areas should have been at the heart of the economic debates surrounding the single currency on continental Europe too.

What does an optimal currency mean? In theory, it would be possible to have a single world currency and, in many respects, the gold standard came close to being such a currency at one time. If we had a single world currency, however, the gains from reduced transactions costs by adding some of the countries would be minimal. At the same time, there could be economic costs from countries joining a single currency area. If the additional countries had rigid labour and product markets and those countries were hit by an economic shock, they would not be able to adjust rapidly to that shock and unemployment might result. If countries keep their own currency, on the other hand, exchange rate flexibility can facilitate economic adjustment. Given this, a case can be made that currency areas can become too big. At the other end of the scale, it would not be efficient for every person in the world to have a separate currency – the transactions costs would be huge. Optimal currency area theory indicates the sort of economic factors we should examine before concluding that countries should – or should not – share a single currency.

Jamie Dannhauser argues that, in continental Europe, political considerations triumphed over economic considerations. Unlike in the UK, the debate about the economics of the euro zone was never predominant. Some economists did argue, however, that, once the euro zone was formed, economic convergence would follow. In that sense an optimal currency area would be endogenous. It would be possible to force countries into a single currency zone and they would then develop the characteristics of an optimal currency area. Jamie Dannhauser demonstrates how that has not happened in practice. Furthermore, he makes a compelling case that there were certain features of countries' financial systems, and their interaction inside the EMU, that have not been considered in the optimal currency area literature. One consequence was the build-up of huge financial imbalances which lay at the heart of the crisis.

The source of the financial imbalances was, in fact, different in different countries. Greece had a profligate government; Ireland, Portugal and Spain, on the other hand, had huge private sector borrowing. This is a key argument – and one that has been glossed over in much of the popular discussion. The banking crisis was more a consequence than a cause of the problems in the euro zone, Dannhauser argues. The underlying cause was the emergence of enormous debt positions in certain countries – in some cases private, in others government – in the context of massive external imbalances between creditor and debtor countries. For example, as Dannhauser comments:

> [N]et borrowing by households and non-financial companies in Spain and Ireland peaked at 14 per cent and 12 per cent of GDP respectively. In Ireland, it was driven mainly by households and an explosion in residential mortgage debt. By contrast, Spanish non-financial corporations were the primary driver of private sector borrowing, although by 2007 households were also running a financial deficit equal to 3 per cent of GDP.

It is quite possible for such imbalances to build up naturally. A country can borrow from abroad, build up a trade deficit, improve its productive capacity and repay borrowings at a later date. It would not be surprising if countries such as Spain and Portugal were to do this in a process of catch-up growth. Dannhauser provides evidence to suggest, however, that this benign process played only a limited role. Instead, the single monetary policy of the ECB interacted with very different financial systems to produce major variations in domestic monetary conditions in different EU countries. In some, this led to a huge explosion in private sector – and in some cases government sector – indebtedness. This, in turn, led to higher spending and inflation in these countries. When these capital flows reversed it was necessary for domestic prices and wages to fall in Ireland, Spain, Italy, Portugal and Greece, in the absence of currency flexibility, in order to generate the export surpluses necessary to repay their foreign borrowing. Without such internal deflation, the drop in domestic consumption caused by the reduction in borrowing from other euro zone states would simply cause unemployment. Ireland is the only one of the periphery states whose economy has shown the flexibility to adapt to the changing circumstances. In particular, relative unit labour costs have fallen there markedly. The other countries are in serious economic trouble that does not look like abating.

There are two very important conclusions from the chapter by Jamie Dannhauser. First, there is a gap in the optimal currency area literature. When economists are considering whether a particular group of countries should share a single currency, they should look at how their banking and financial systems might interact. If they do not consider this, credit and capital flows within those systems might cause economic dislocation and be a source of economic shocks that affect different countries in different ways. Secondly, as the optimal currency area literature suggests, countries need to have flexible labour and product markets in order to adjust to economic shocks. Politics was at the heart of the decision to form the single currency, but even the most optimistic interpretation of the economic case ignored these important points. The weight of evidence, argues Jamie Dannhauser, suggests that the EMU cannot survive without a radical overhaul.

The middle

Moving on from the causes of the current crisis, John Chown considers the troubles of the euro zone in a historical context by examining previous monetary unions. He finds that history suggests that monetary unions will not survive unless they are the precursor to political unions. Without political union it is very difficult to ensure that each country maintains fiscal discipline and that each state is responsible for its own debts. Interstate transfers and the socialisation of debt are also politically very difficult. Though the continental liberal economists may be correct in theory, Chown argues that it is impossible in practice to create the kind of monetary union that they desire.

John Chown suggests that Greece should have been allowed to leave the euro much earlier in the crisis and that allowing Greece to remain in the euro has been costly. The authorities are arguing that they will pay 'whatever it costs' to save the euro but, logically, there are only two sources of money. One is the surplus countries, of which Germany is by far the biggest; the other is through money creation, which would impose costs on all savers and will, in any case, be blocked by Germany.

Most UK economists would argue that there was far too little serious economic analysis before countries joined the euro. If there is a move to a new, slimmed-down euro zone, countries should examine very carefully the costs and benefits of joining and, in particular, examine the fiscal balance sheets of the different countries with which they would be unifying their currencies. The long-term fiscal position depends on pension liabilities and the extent to which pension provision is privately funded. This is an issue that has largely been ignored but could yet break the euro if it survives the current crisis.

Just because it might have been better if the euro had never been created (though not all the authors of this monograph would accept that premise), it does not follow that, in the midst of the crisis, it should be abandoned. The chapters by Lilico, and by Schwartz, Cabrillo and Castañeda, examine the question of whether euro zone countries should exit.

Andrew Lilico discusses how imbalances built up in the euro zone. Specifically there were some natural shifts in relative competitiveness that always occur within currency zones – relative prices never remain constant in an economy; secondly, there were mistaken assumptions made about the relative future growth and stability of different euro zone regions which led to excessive capital flows; thirdly, there were unsustainable government debt accumulation policies.

The situation that the euro zone found itself in in 2009 meant that significant adjustments in relative labour costs were needed between some countries in order to restore competitiveness. In Ireland significant adjustments have already occurred, though there needs to be more adjustment in other indebted countries. Lilico suggests that floating exchange rates are more effective at facilitating adjustment at lower cost for a variety of reasons: there are fewer frictional costs of relative price movements; sticky prices can lead to prolonged unemployment when depreciation is not possible; and debt servicing can be more problematic in an environment of internal devaluation.

In the case of Ireland, however, Andrew Lilico demonstrates that the additional costs of economic adjustment that tend to exist under fixed exchange rates have probably already been borne. In the case of other countries, there may still be long-term benefits from membership of the euro zone – most particularly because membership is encouraging reform by those governments. As such, it does not follow that exit, now we are in the midst of the crisis, is necessary, desirable, or is going to be politically possible. In the case of Ireland, perhaps the right moment for exit has passed. In the case of the Mediterranean countries, it might be desirable to use the straitjacket of the euro to encourage economic reform and then exit.

Andrew Lilico argues convincingly that, if the euro zone is to survive, there must, under no circumstances, be a debt union (a recurring theme in this monograph), although some fiscal transfers are justified. Schwartz, Cabrillo and Castañeda point out that, although euro members cannot exit the euro, they can be suspended. Suspension of a member, such as Greece, would involve substantial costs because, realistically, the euro value of the euro-denominated bank deposits of Greek citizens would have to be guaranteed whereas international loans to Greek citizens and corporations would have to be denominated in a 'new drachma'. There are also huge costs, however, involved in maintaining the status quo. The authors point out that the direct costs include the loans to bail out Greece (€240 billion committed), Ireland (€67.5 billion), Portugal (€78 billion) and now Spanish banks (€100 billion committed), as well as costs implicit in the debt guarantees offered by the EU of more than €600 billion. In addition, the ECB has greatly expanded and will go on expanding its balance sheet by purchasing bonds of doubtful quality. It has also promised to buy sovereign debt on the secondary market, with the pretext that the ensuing interest rate reductions would increase the efficiency of the monetary policy transmission mechanism.

Any resolution of the Greek crisis requires creditors to recognise the reality that there will be a substantial default on government debt. The authors suggest, however, that private sector mechanisms would be much more effective at dealing with such default than governmental or EU mechanisms. The World Debt Corporation, the Paris Club (for sovereign creditors) and the London Club (for private creditors) should be the main points of focus for debt resolution. After all, since the mid-1950s, the Paris Club has assisted in sovereign debt restructuring of more than eighty countries through more than four hundred agreements covering more than $550 billion.

... and the end?

Like Dickens's *Great Expectations* this story has two possible endings – a 'sad' one and an ambiguous one (or, perhaps more accurately, the monograph has an unfortunate ending and a series of alternative consistent policy choices).

The unfortunate ending would be the continuation of the status quo.

Youth unemployment in Greece is now 58 per cent; general unemployment in Spain is 27 per cent and poverty and inequality both seem to be increasing. The reaction to the crisis has been to socialise responsibility for sovereign and banking debts and to centralise regulation further – especially in the financial sector. From the point of view of the promotion of a market economy, the continuation of current policy is a disaster.

The alternative policy choices all, in their own way, impose discipline on and curtail the powers of government or promote decentralisation and a market economy. All would involve the end of the euro zone as we know it, though not all would involve the end of the euro.

Parallel currencies[1]

Schwartz, Cabrillo and Castañeda argue in favour of parallel currencies as a stable, long-term solution to the euro crisis. Suspended members should be allowed to issue their own parallel currencies alongside the euro. The ECB should become fully independent and those members that want a sound euro – and do not wish to have their own parallel currencies – should demand monetary management along classical lines from the ECB.

The authors state:

> With a parallel currency regime, residents, banks and governments would still be able to use the euro. Commercial banks especially would keep their connection with the ECB as well as with the new drachma central bank: i.e. both central banks would act as lenders of last resort along Bagehot lines. Neither currency needs to be

---

1   The use of parallel currencies was proposed by the UK government in the run-up to the creation of the euro. That proposal is discussed in the chapter by John Chown. Philip Booth and Alberto Mingardi proposed parallel currencies as a solution to the euro zone crisis in early 2011 in an article in the *Wall Street Journal*. See: http://online.wsj.com/article/SB10001424052748703583404576079783584813132.html. The proposal in this chapter, however, is thought through in more detail and is related to the legal provisions of the treaties establishing the euro.

legal tender. European politicians and officials, however, will want
to reject this solution of floating parallel currencies for its apparent
untidiness, for fear of competitive devaluations and because 'it has
never been tried'.

It would be important, under this settlement, that euro and drachma
freely float and that neither has legal tender status. Both the Bank of
Greece and the ECB would have incentives to manage their currencies
soundly in order to obtain seigniorage. The possibility of a member
exiting and issuing a parallel currency, however, would take the pressure
off the European monetary institutions and resolve tensions between
member states. It would also ensure that countries could have the necessary currency flexibility to deal with asymmetric economic shocks.
Furthermore, the euro zone could evolve back into a single currency area
through the free choice of individuals and businesses.

A return to national currencies

Neil Record suggests winding up the euro altogether. He argues that the
ECB is effectively supporting the European banking system and thus it
has gone a long way beyond its remit of setting monetary policy in the
euro zone. The ECB is now providing core funding to a large number of
euro zone banks that cannot fund themselves except at ruinously high
interest rates (if at all). The liabilities on the Eurosystem balance sheet
at 15 June 2012 stood at €3.03 trillion or 32 per cent of annual euro zone
GDP. Record argues that this is an alarmingly large number for a thinly
capitalised multilateral institution, with vulnerable sovereign assets. This,
together with the fact that the euro prevents sovereign countries from
pursuing monetary policies that are appropriate to their own circumstances, means that the euro has, in effect, reached the end of the road.

The practical problems of winding the euro up, however, would
be immense. Among other problems, there will be billions of euros of
contracts operating under non-euro-zone law, which will continue, in

the legal sense, to be obligations of the contracting parties. Neil Record suggests that the European Currency Unit (ECU) would need to be re-created in order to provide a basis for settling these debts.

Record directly challenges pro-euro continental liberal economists by arguing that a strong advantage of the winding up of the euro will be that each country's politicians will only have to account for their performance to their own electorate – not to another layer of government in Brussels.

It is extremely important that a tariff-free market remains intact in the EU, and Record points out that there is no reason why this cannot continue with all 27 countries having individual currencies. Specifically he argues that, in the wake of euro break-up:

> If we are to avoid a full-blown depression, then it is vital that, in
> the wake of this enormous political and economic convulsion, the
> energising force of international trade, and its positive effect on the
> welfare and wealth of nations, is allowed to flourish. This will be
> the challenge for a new generation of post-euro politicians.

Neil Record warns that euro break-up will not happen through the choice of the euro zone elite but through *force majeure* of some description. Nevertheless, a plan has to be carefully worked out and followed through to ensure that economic chaos does not result.

Sound governance and a reformed euro

Bodo Herzog and Katja Hengstermann argue that the euro can thrive if the founding principles are reinforced. There were, they remind us, rules created to ensure that countries remained disciplined in their approach to government spending and taxation. Unfortunately, these rules have been violated. If the rules had been obeyed and there was no prospect of bailouts, the incentives would have existed for member countries to reform their economies in other ways to bring the euro zone closer to an optimal currency area.

The authors argue that the rules by which the member states should operate should be completely clear – there should be no ambiguity whatsoever. They then propose a new approach to disciplining members. First, if a country violated the debt, deficit and other public spending conditions for membership of the euro, it would gradually lose voting rights in Ecofin, thus, in effect, losing any influence over the EU budget. Persistent violations would lead to expulsion from the decision-making mechanisms of the euro zone. Effectively, in this case, a country would become 'euroised' (i.e. using euros as if they were a foreign currency). Alternatively, countries could be suspended from the euro altogether until they met the necessary conditions. Furthermore, the extent of countries' fiscal autonomy would depend on how close they came to meeting the *ex ante* rules. While many readers of this monograph may wish to see the euro zone dissolved, this proposal should not be dismissed. Effectively, the euro zone would be treated as a club with clear rules for membership.

Free banking and the end of nationalised currencies

The proposal of Herzog and Hengstermann does seek to decouple the euro from political management by limiting discretion. It nevertheless would remain a single currency with the decision-taking mechanisms being tied up with member governments. The final proposal is for an end to the link between politics and the management of monetary policy altogether. Kevin Dowd proposes a free banking solution to the euro zone's monetary problems.

Dowd suggests that his proposal is idealistic – European monetary union was, however, at one time, idealistic too. Just as the euro seems not to have succeeded, state currencies have also not been a great success in that they have tended to suffer from high rates of inflation. On the other hand, there is, argues Dowd, a successful history of free banking, not least in Scotland.[2] Unlike systems with state-controlled currencies, free banking systems prevent governments funding their activities through monetary finance and provide strong incentives for currency-issuing banks to behave prudently. Of course, there is potentially a loss of network benefits from free banking systems especially if there are competing units of account, but, with electronic means of payment, perhaps these are less important.

These four proposals all involve some combination of decentralisation; mechanisms to ensure that governments are held to their promises; competition; or a greater direct role for the market economy. As such, they are surely based on a sounder foundation than a euro system in which huge monetary transfers are taking place underwritten by the taxpayers of the least indebted nations.

References

Issing, O. (2000), *Hayek, Currency Competition and European Monetary Union*, Occasional Paper 111, London: Institute of Economic Affairs.

Minford, P. (2002), *Should Britain Join the Euro? The Chancellor's Five Tests Examined*, Occasional Paper 126, London: Institute of Economic Affairs.

2   Interestingly, Scotland is currently preparing to hold a referendum on independence from the United Kingdom. Those proposing independence have accepted that Scotland will not use the euro in the short term and the UK Chancellor of the Exchequer has indicated that Scotland will not be part of the UK monetary policy and central banking system. If that is the case, then Scotland may have to pursue some kind of currency board arrangement, 'sterlingisation' or 'euroisation', which would take it closer to a free banking system than any current EU member.

2 BRITAIN AND THE EURO ZONE
   – A TRIUMPH OF ECONOMICS OVER POLITICS

Patrick Minford[1]

The euro project and the UK's national interest

The project to create the euro is having a massive effect on the evolution of the European Union, both economically and politically. The British refusal to join was based on economic criteria – colloquially known as the 'five tests' set by the Treasury under Gordon Brown's Chancellorship, and reported on in HM Treasury (2003). The refusal of the UK to join the euro, however, will surely also turn out to have major political implications for our relationship with the EU.

In this chapter, I will begin by reviewing why the UK refused to join the euro and the arguments put on both sides. Then I will consider how the euro has turned out and how those arguments look today in the light of those developments. Finally, I will turn to the implications for the UK of the likely evolution of the euro zone within the EU.

The case for the euro and the UK's decision not to join

The reasoning behind the creation of the euro on the continent was largely political: to create an instrument for forging greater political union or, as some French supporters put it, *'Europe par la monnaie'*. German participation was reluctant in terms of economic considerations alone, since the Deutschmark was to be surrendered, but Germany was enthusiastic in terms of the politics. An indication of how subordinate the economic case for the euro was in continental Europe is that the sole

---

1   I am grateful for helpful comments from referees.

economic analysis of its effects was put out as an issue of the European Commission's *Economic Bulletin*. Nevertheless, opposition by economists on the continent was muted; free market economists in Germany thought that competitive pressures would force economic reform on southern Europe, while economists in the south welcomed the infusion of northern discipline on their unruly politics. When some German economists' opposition finally reached the Constitutional Court in Karlsruhe in 1998, it was far too late and the court refused to block the euro.

From the UK's viewpoint, political union was not generally desired and so the arguments about joining were purely economic. I argued in work at the time (Minford, 2002; Minford et al., 2004) that there was a strong case against the UK joining; this view was widely shared by British industrialists, as became clear when both the Institute of Directors and the CBI came out against joining in the wake of a strong campaign mounted by Business for Sterling. Nevertheless, the political case held strong appeal for 'New Labour' politicians, presumably because they felt it would entrench continental-style social democracy in the UK, as Margaret Thatcher put it, 'through the back door'. Thus Tony Blair said in his 2002 New Year message (Blair, 2001): 'The New Year sees the introduction of the European single currency. With so much of our trade and so many of our jobs tied up in business with the rest of Europe, it is massively in our interests that the euro succeeds. It remains the government's policy to join the euro provided that the five economic tests we have laid down are met and the British people give their consent in a referendum', and earlier (Blair, 1998): 'The decision to launch the single currency is the first step and marks the turning point for Europe, marks stability and growth and is crucial to high levels of growth and employment.' With such strong political backing from the British prime minister of the time it took a serious political struggle, led ironically by Labour's Chancellor but crucially allied, as we have seen, to the mass of UK business opinion, organised by Business for Sterling, to stop the UK joining this ill-fated enterprise.

The economic arguments for joining revolved around the reduction of costs in exchanging currency: see, for example, Barrell (2002), Barrell and Dury (2000), Britain in Europe (2000) and EU Commission (1990). Of these, the transactions costs of currency exchange of sterling with the existing EU currencies were widely agreed to be trivial and increasingly carried out through the banking system. They were essentially offset by the cost of change-over to a new currency. A related cost, of cross-border price non-transparency, was also trivial for the UK with its lack of active borders with the euro zone. The cost of bilateral exchange rate uncertainty was, however, potentially serious; the cost of insuring against this acts like a tax on bilateral trade and capital movements. Nevertheless, this bilateral cost is simply one source of currency uncertainty; the UK faces currency uncertainty in relation to other bilateral transactions, most importantly in dollars, and this would not disappear because joining the euro would be a move to join a regional currency not a world currency. Roughly speaking, a little under half of the UK's foreign exchange dealings were with EU currencies, and a little over half with the rest of the world (essentially the dollar or currencies linked to the dollar with varying degrees of closeness). There was a high degree of volatility in the dollar exchange rate with EU currencies (see Figure 1, which shows the dollar against the Deutschmark before January 1999 and the euro afterwards; the sterling real effective exchange rate is shown alongside). This is a continuing feature of the international economy, as these two continents do not coordinate their monetary policies closely, if at all. In these circumstances, by joining the euro the UK would exacerbate its volatility against the dollar, whereas if it remained unattached to either currency its average movement would respond to UK shocks, much as, in practice, the sterling real exchange rate seems to have done, as shown in Figure 1. Simulation analysis by my research team suggested that, overall, joining the euro would create as much currency uncertainty against the dollar as it would eliminate against the euro, giving no overall gain from reduced uncertainty. Thus the main argument for joining the regional euro currency had no traction for the UK.

The arguments against joining the euro fell into three main

Figure 1 **The euro–dollar and the sterling real effective exchange rate**
1990 = 100

Source: published exchange rates, consumer prices and author's calculations

categories. The first was the macroeconomic volatility that would be induced by giving up control over monetary policy to the European Central Bank (ECB) with its euro-wide mandate. Outside the euro, UK monetary policy could respond to UK conditions and stabilise them; inside the euro, they could not. Furthermore, inside the euro the UK economy would be vulnerable to movements in euro interest rates and the euro exchange rate against the dollar, produced by euro zone shocks: these movements would be equivalent to extra shocks to the UK economy. This argument echoes the traditional 'optimal currency area' arguments well known in the currency literature. The team were finding from our modelling work that the UK was highly 'asymmetric' – that is, prone to shocks different from those affecting the euro zone. The quantitative estimates we made at the time indicated that our economy would suffer from roughly double the volatility it would have had outside the euro: for the details, see Minford (2002).

The second category concerned bailout. The Maastricht Treaty outlawed any bailouts of countries in the euro zone by other countries; supposedly the Stability and Growth Pact would buttress the treaty in this respect. Few UK observers felt that this was credible, and our work outlined various ways in which large-scale transfers might be induced, especially as further integration took place. We focused on the pressures from ageing populations and consequent age-related government expenditure; but, as we have seen, the banking crisis has produced another more immediate source of transfer pressure.

The third category concerned regulation. This is an argument peculiarly related to the EU. It seemed to the opponents of UK membership of the euro zone that the zone would develop its own regulatory approach because euro zone members would perceive a need for uniformity in order to strengthen the institutions of the single currency. This approach would spill over into the EU's general institutions because the euro zone's members are in a large majority within the EU. We argued that this would be a source of further excessive regulation, already identified by us as a general cost of EU membership.

In our quantitative assessment of these factors, we found that all three of these problems were potentially serious for the UK. We calculated that on entry, as noted above, UK macroeconomic volatility would roughly double; that the costs of potential transfers could reach 9 per cent of GDP on worst-case scenarios; and that the regulatory burden of EU membership would be worsened to a degree that was hard to assess but possibly costing up to 25 per cent of GDP (a recent study, Congdon, 2012, puts the total cost of EU membership at 10 per cent of GDP, which is of a similar order to the bottom end of our estimates shown in Table 1). As the benefits from joining in terms of reduced currency uncertainty were nil because of our trade with the dollar area, there was an unambiguous and strong case against joining. This, of course, was also the view of HM Treasury on the basis of the 'five tests', which were Whitehall's version of a cost–benefit study along the lines of optimal currency area analysis; and so the UK did not join. This now seems a providentially wise decision, in the light of events since the banking crisis erupted – a topic we turn to next.

The euro zone in the light of events

The banking crisis led to the crisis within the euro zone, in which the fiscal and balance of payments difficulties of the southern countries caused their sovereign debt to be reassessed. This in turn led to southern banks' solvency being reassessed since they in turn were major holders of their countries' sovereign debt.

How did all this come about? Before the crisis these countries ran systematically large current account deficits as their rapid growth sucked in imports and generated relatively high inflation, eroding the competitiveness of their export and import-substitute industries. These deficits were financed by capital inflows, mainly private bank lending, intermediating the savings of the slow-growing north into loans to the south.

When the crisis hit, the southern countries' growth rate suffered and this reduced their imports; their exports also suffered from slow world growth, however, and their current account deficits were not much reduced. Furthermore, their public deficits worsened, as revenues fell and spending did not. Concerns began to grow that foreign debt, both to the private and public sectors, would not be serviced. This meant that capital inflows required a much higher return to compensate for the growing risks; these increased risk premia began with Greece but soon spread to other southern countries.

At this point we need to focus on the behaviour of the ECB and its component central banks. Faced with the spiralling costs of foreign lending, local banks in the south turned to their central banks for finance, as they were entitled to through the ECB's discount window. Very large amounts of euros were lent to local banks by this means, essentially replacing the capital inflow via the market. By this indirect route the north found itself lending large amounts to the south via the ECB – these amounts are known as 'Target 2 Balances' because Target is the acronym for the intra-central-bank settlement system in the euro zone. Of course, effectively settlement has been suspended since this crisis process got under way because there is no possibility of southern central banks 'settling' with northern central banks in the euro system.

This ECB-mediated rescue mechanism for the south is the key to understanding how the euro is developing. The amount involved had reached around one trillion euros by late 2012 – far in excess of the official rescue funds being discussed at euro zone summits. It has the potential to rise much further as euros flee the afflicted southern banking system and current account deficits continue.

Because the ECB can act in this way, something that was not generally predicted before the crisis, the likelihood of euro break-up is much diminished. As is well known, southern populaces are against leaving the euro by large majorities because of the fear of the economic and political chaos that could ensue. This means that one of the northern countries would have to pull out for the euro to collapse. If, for example, Germany were to do so, however, it would involve potentially sacrificing most of these large debts contracted by southern banks. Such losses act as a deterrent to pulling out, in addition to the usual factors cited, such as fear in Germany that the Deutschmark would appreciate sharply or that European solidarity would be damaged.

In turn, the continued survival of the euro means that we could be facing a decade or so of intermittent crisis in the euro zone as new institutions are put into place to satisfy the demands of Germany and the north in return for their assistance to the south.

These dramatic developments have clearly reinforced the case for the UK not joining the euro. With the euro the UK would be vulnerable to the same pressures that have worsened the crisis in the south. Unable to control its own monetary policy, the UK would be unable to allow the pound to float downwards, which can facilitate an improvement in net exports, nor could it generate government debt on the scale it has with quantitative easing, bolstering the prices of gilts against panic sales such as have occurred with Italy and Spain and reducing long-term interest rates. The UK recession, which has been bad enough because of the severity of the banking crisis generally, could have been worsened on the scale of southern countries, where growth has been heavily negative and continues to be so, with unemployment reaching record rates.

To understand just how its floating exchange rate has enabled the UK to avoid the sort of run on government debt that has occurred in the south, consider what would happen were UK gilts to be subject to a drop in foreign buying owing to a temporary perception of increased sovereign default risk among foreign buyers of gilts – a run on gilts that is due to a 'panic' for some reason. Considering this from the perspective of a US investor, we would expect sterling to depreciate until the expected return on UK government bonds in dollars was equal to the return on US Treasuries. Hence the higher temporary risk premium would be offset by a lower sterling exchange rate. This lower exchange rate improves economic growth prospects, supporting the prospects for public finances. Furthermore, the Bank of England is free to buy gilts in exchange for money, further underpinning the gilt price. Gilt yields need not change significantly, the Treasury needs to make no cuts in spending to offset rising yields, and the panic subsides. Any gilt purchases by the central bank can then be reversed.

Compare this with the situation in, say, Italy. If Italian treasury bonds are seen as risky for some reason, they are sold for other euro-denominated bonds until their yield rises (their prices fall) to compensate for the higher risk. This then implies that the Italian treasury must find more spending cuts to pay the higher yields on newly issued debt; as this is difficult, the risk perception rises further, causing the problem to worsen. Economic prospects also worsen as interest rates rise across the economy, further damaging government revenues. The 'run' becomes self-fulfilling. Until the ECB announced its new policy of Outright Monetary Transactions, whereby it would support government bond prices if there were seen to be such a run, there was chaos in these southern markets, fuelling the euro zone crisis. Even now there is some uncertainty about how far the ECB would or could go with this policy in the face of a serious crisis of confidence in a southern country.

Furthermore, even if the UK had managed to avoid this southern-style fate, it too, like Germany and other northern countries, would have been forced to make large-scale transfers to stricken southern countries. The bailout issue, which was denied as a problem by the proponents of the euro, has clearly been a major problem in practice. Germans believed that they would not be called upon to make transfers to other euro zone countries, thus joining a 'transfer zone'. They were wrong.

In sum, the euro zone crisis is likely to continue for a number of years, until a new institutional framework is agreed that sufficiently reassures northern Europe that its transfers to southern Europe will have a good chance of being repaid. The UK's exclusion has meant that it is neither vulnerable to the panic that has engulfed southern sovereign bonds nor is it in line to make transfers to the crisis-stricken south.

The evolution of the EU during this crisis and its effect on the UK

The institutional framework being developed implies a high degree of monitoring and intervention within the euro zone. There will be controls on bank behaviour, targets for governments and new financial taxes. While in principle this will take place within the euro zone, there will be pressure to extend it to all EU countries on the grounds that other EU members could 'undercut' euro zone arrangements. The UK will be seen as an offshore competitor for those banks, businesses and governments in the zone that are burdened with these controls and regulations. It will be argued that such competition will be unfair under the single market regime, for which qualified majority voting applies. It would be easy to extend proposed new regulations to the UK by majority or qualified majority vote.

Furthermore, the pressures for protection will increase in order to produce as much euro zone growth as possible, for best prospects of debt repayment. Serious recessions for long periods such as that which the euro zone is undergoing make such pressures intense. The UK suffers at present from the protectionism that is imposed by the EU as a whole. This protection will probably increase; even within the EU covert protection against non-euro countries could occur.

At best, the euro zone will be obsessed with the euro crisis for the coming decade, stalling any progress in liberalising markets and increasing competition – things that would benefit the UK; indeed, they would benefit the whole EU.

This tendency for the euro to strengthen the impetus towards excessive regulation as a way of bolstering the single currency was foreseen at the introduction of the euro. But the crisis is likely to make this tendency much stronger.

For the UK this prospect is extremely damaging. Even without any change in the status quo, the economic costs to the UK of being in the EU are substantial: Table 1 summarises the estimates made by Minford et al. (2005). Even though they assume that the UK remains outside the euro, with the changes the euro crisis threatens, they will increase towards the upper end of the possible spectrum identified in our original work.

Table 1 **A conspectus of costs from being in the EU (% of GDP)**

Net UK contribution	0.4
Common Agricultural Policy	0.3
Manufacturing trade protectionism	2.5–3
Harmonisation of regulation	6–25
Potential transfer costs*	2–9
Total	11.2–37.7

*These consist of bailout transfers, either because of crises such as the present one or future pension problems.
Source: Minford et al. (2005)

A contrary and popular argument is that there are offsetting benefits of EU membership to the UK as a result of foreign direct investment (FDI) (for example, see NIESR, 2000). This argument is entirely

fallacious, however. FDI brings benefits because of technological spillo-
vers from foreign firms, which raise productivity. It is true that FDI has
taken place in such industries as motor manufacturing, where the UK
was inefficient, and has brought benefits. If the UK left the EU, however,
and in the absence of trade protectionism from the EU traded goods
prices fell to world price levels, then UK comparative advantage would
dominate industrial development, and where there were gains from FDI
in the industries favoured by this comparative advantage, FDI would
switch to these industries. If, on the other hand, these industries were
already at the technological frontier, then FDI would bring no gains:
FDI is beneficial only if the industrial environment is inefficient. The
UK economy's productivity is likely to be maximised when comparative
advantage is allowed its fullest rein, i.e. under free trade. If this structure
implies that industries operating in the UK are more efficient, then less
FDI will be required. But this will reflect the fact that the UK is more
productive, not less. In other words, FDI is an input, not a measure of
the UK's productivity performance. Free trade should maximise the UK's
productivity, regardless of how much FDI it generates.

Thus the costs to the UK of being in the EU are already high and are
likely to increase under the pressure of the euro crisis. This implies that
the case for leaving the EU will become even stronger, to the point where
it overcomes the force of inertia from the status quo. A referendum on
renegotiation or on departure if renegotiation is denied will become difficult to avoid. As can be seen from the figures quoted above, in any case
total departure is the desirable option, while maintaining some arrangements on particular issues of common interest, such as rights of migra-
tion, free capital movements and possibly trade agreements in particular
industries such as motor manufacturing where there is large-scale cross-
investment. Clearly, as in most reforms that improve general welfare
at the cost of damage to special interests, some transitional arrangements and other compensation will be needed for those who lose from
the change, principally industries protected by the EU customs union.
These are by now only a small percentage of UK GDP, however, given

the contraction of our manufacturing industry in the face of shifting comparative advantage within the world economy. Any budgetary transfers would be small, especially once EU transitional arrangements have been agreed.

Conclusions

The UK's decision not to join the euro was taken on purely economic grounds. These grounds related to the increased volatility of the economy, the costs of bailout and the risk of greater regulatory intrusion. The gains from eliminating euro currency risk were offset by the extra currency risk against dollar-related currencies. Since the banking crisis and the resulting euro zone crisis, it has become apparent that all these problems were even bigger than we thought then: volatility could be far greater, as demonstrated by the experiences of southern countries; bailouts could be enormous, as Germany is finding; and the evolving institutional structure of the euro zone is likely to spawn far more intrusive regulation for the EU as a whole. In previous work my co-authors and I found that EU membership imposed substantial net economic costs on the UK; the institutional evolution being triggered by the euro crisis threatens to make these costs higher still, in a highly visible way. It seems likely that it will lead to a major political reassessment of the UK's relationship with the EU.

References

Barrell, R. (2002), 'The UK and EMU: choosing the regime', *National Institute Economic Review*, 180(1): 54–71.

Barrell, R. and K. Dury (2000), 'Choosing the regime: macroeconomic effects of UK entry into the EU', *Journal of Common Market Studies*, 38(4): 625–44.

Blair, T. (1998, 2001), quotations from 'Key quotes from Tony Blair on the euro', Guardian online, 16 May 2002.

Britain in Europe (2000), *The Case for the Euro*, London: Britain in Europe.

Congdon, T. (2012), *How Much Does the European Union Cost Britain?*, London: UKIP.

Emerson, M., D. Gros and A. Italianer (1990), *One Market One Money – An Evaluation of the Potential Benefits and Costs of Forming an Economic and Monetary Union*, New York: Oxford University Press.

European Commission (1990), 'One market one money: an evaluation of the potential benefits and costs of forming an economic and monetary union', *European Economy*, 44, October.

HM Treasury (2003), *UK Membership of the Single Currency – an Assessment of the Five Economic Tests*, Cm 5776, June.

Minford, P. (2002), *Should Britain Join the Euro? The Chancellor's Five Tests Examined*, Occasional Paper 126, London: Institute of Economic Affairs.

Minford, P., V. Mahambare and E. Nowell (2005), *Should Britain Leave the EU?: An Economic Analysis of a Troubled Relationship*, London: Edward Elgar and the Institute of Economic Affairs.

Minford, P., D. Meenagh and B. Webb (2004), 'Britain and EMU: assessing the costs in macroeconomic variability', *World Economy*, 27(3): 301–58.

NIESR (2000), 'Continent cut off? The macroeconomic impact of British withdrawal from the EU', *NIESR Review*, February.

3 THE EURO – THE STORY OF A SUBOPTIMAL CURRENCY AREA

Jamie Dannhauser

'There is no example in history of a lasting monetary union that was not linked to one State.'

OTMAR ISSING, CHIEF ECONOMIST OF THE BUNDESBANK,
1991

Introduction

Nearly four years after the collapse of Lehman Brothers, the global financial system is still under immense strain. While turmoil in the euro zone is the proximate cause of recent dislocations, the financial imbalances and distortions in the global economy that built up during the 'Goldilocks era' are the root of the problem. They are still a long way from being resolved. At the height of the financial crisis, G20 leaders were able to find common ground – aggressive policy stimulus to prevent a rerun of the 1930s was in everyone's interest. Three years on, that sense of common purpose has been lost. A major adjustment in the pattern of global demand and output is necessary, if the world economy is to return to a stable growth path. To be successful, it requires the cooperation of *both* debtor and creditor nations. Retrenchment in one must be offset by reflation in the other. Asymmetric adjustment is likely to be self-defeating, resulting in materially weaker output growth, if not global recession.

In many ways, the euro zone is a microcosm of the world at large. Its problems centre on external imbalances that cannot be resolved by one-sided adjustment. For the moment, the ECB's generous liquidity support to euro zone banks, its promise of unlimited Spanish and Italian

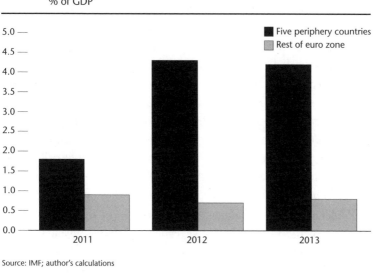

Figure 2   **Size of euro area fiscal consolidation**
            % of GDP

Source: IMF; author's calculations

sovereign bond purchases subject to Troika oversight, and international bailout packages for Greece, Portugal and Ireland have prevented an even more severe income collapse in periphery economies; but creditor nations are doing little to help in actively rebalancing domestic demand in the euro area (see Figure 2).

In May 2012, Sir Mervyn King, governor of the Bank of England, suggested that 'the euro area ... was tearing itself apart without any obvious solution'. This chapter will explain why the structure of Economic and Monetary Union (EMU) itself laid the foundations for the crisis which now threatens its future, and why that structure will have to be significantly strengthened and potentially redesigned. It should be noted that monetary union was, and still is, a political project, but this chapter will stray only briefly into those political areas.

Moreover, we should not be blind to the fact that the euro zone crisis is taking place against the backdrop of the most severe banking disruption in over a century. Powerful global forces exaggerated the financial imbalances inside the euro zone and now condition the wider economic environment in which their unwinding is taking place. These include, but are not limited to, the following: an *ex ante* excess of global savings over global investment, which put sustained downward pressure on world equilibrium real interest rates (see Bernanke, 2005); the particular choice of 'risk-free' US dollar debt as the vehicle for many countries' currency management and foreign exchange accumulation, which depressed term premia along the US yield curve (see Warnock, 2006, or Tucker, 2012); the 'search for yield' and compression of risk premia in credit markets (see Borio and Disyatat, 2011); excessive risk-taking by banks because of unduly low central bank policy rates, the so-called 'risk-taking channel of monetary policy' (see Borio and Zhu, 2008, or Altunbas et al., 2010); and extensive regulatory arbitrage in and lax regulation of the banking industry.

In the popular debate, there has been considerable focus on excessive government debts and deficits in the euro area. A failure of the Stability and Growth Pact (SGP) to discipline member nations' fiscal behaviour is widely seen as a major contributor to the euro zone's current problems. The proposed cure has been strengthened oversight of EMU members' budgetary positions in the longer term and intense pressure to reduce fiscal deficits in the immediate future, hence the asymmetric adjustment just referred to. For some countries, most notably Greece, this is justified. But to suggest that fiscal profligacy is the main cause of the euro zone's ills is to misunderstand the problem (see Figure 3). In both Spain and Ireland, increasing external imbalances were mirrored in a growing *private* sector financial deficit, and coincided with budget surpluses and falling public sector debt. Meanwhile, both Germany and the Netherlands breached the SGP's 3 per cent of GDP deficit limit (as did France between 2002 and 2004) and ran budget deficits on average from 1999 to 2007, while sustaining large current account surpluses. What unite 'core' and 'periphery' countries are large *external* surpluses and deficits respectively, and the net foreign asset/liability positions that arose as a result.

Figure 3 **General government net debt in 2007**
% of GDP, IMF data

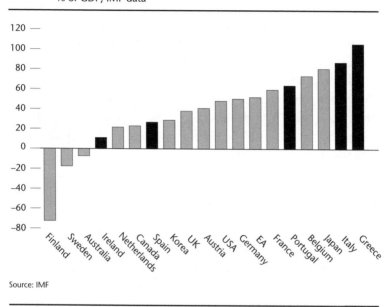

Source: IMF

Increasing external imbalances may have had their genesis in funda-mental forces driving savings and investment in euro zone countries. But by the start of the financial crisis, a configuration of unsustainable external positions between EMU members had arisen. If EMU is going to remain intact, its institutional architecture is going to have to be radically altered, since existing arrangements do not provide a credible mechanism for reducing the extreme financial imbalances that built up before 2008. Investors clearly believe there is meaningful risk that at least one country will leave EMU. The steps that need to be taken, at least in broad terms, are fairly clear. Whether these are achievable in the time available given domestic political constraints is another matter. In 'periphery' countries, sustained fiscal retrenchment and disruptive structural reform threaten to undermine support for pro-euro, centrist parties; but there is also a danger for 'core' nations, where political backing for ongoing financing of the periphery may falter. History suggests that economic stagnation and political upheaval are frequent bedfellows. Across Europe, disillusionment with the political process is growing: fewer people are choosing to vote, and those that do are increasingly turning away from the centrist parties that have long dominated European politics. For many, monetary union in Europe was always a stepping stone to political union – Wim Duisenburg, former president of the ECB, made this point openly. But full political and fiscal union may not be feasible in the economic and political reality of the euro zone today.

The theory of optimal currency areas

In light of recent difficulties, it is far from obvious that all seventeen EMU members are better off, economically and politically, inside the euro area. In the jargon, it is time to ask whether EMU is, or can still become, an optimal currency area. Economists define an optimal currency area to be the optimal geographic domain of a single currency, or of several currencies whose exchange rates are irrevocably pegged and might be unified. Optimality is defined in terms of several optimal currency area criteria or properties which will be detailed below. The more that independent sovereigns share these properties, the greater the benefits of operating inside a unified monetary system of nation-states. As long as there are sufficiently powerful mechanisms for real adjustment between nations, there will be limited use for domestic monetary policy and a floating nominal exchange rate to foster internal and external balance.

An implicit assumption in much of the optimal currency area literature is that the nominal exchange rate is a useful macroeconomic stabilisation tool.[1] But, as Buiter (2000) has pointed out, changes in a country's real exchange rate (the nominal exchange rate adjusted for differences

---

1   Throughout, the assumption of a 'small' economy will be maintained, i.e. we abstract from economies, such as the USA, that have sufficient market power to influence prices in world markets for internationally traded goods and services.

in prices/costs between countries) are what foster external adjustment. Therefore, a key judgement is the extent to which independent monetary policy and exchange rate flexibility have lasting effects on activity, via shifts in the real exchange rate. Empirically, this will be determined by the severity of nominal rigidities, i.e. the 'stickiness' of prices and costs. In a world of fully flexible prices and wages, changes in the nominal exchange rate should have no effect on the real exchange rate.

What criteria need to be met for it to be advantageous for countries to form a monetary union and lose the nominal exchange rate as a stabilisation tool? And what other mechanisms are available to allow constituent economies to adjust to country-specific shocks (or common shocks which have idiosyncratic effects)? Firstly, there are *ex ante* forces which should prevent demand deviating too far from potential output, and limit the build-up of unsustainable financial imbalances. Secondly, there are *ex post* mechanisms which aid adjustment over the longer term, if imbalances develop.

Mongelli (2002) provides a useful overview of the standard optimal currency area criteria, which are outlined below.

The degree of nominal rigidities in domestic prices and costs

For the choice of exchange rate regime to matter at all, there must be some inflexibility in the setting of prices and costs. An economy that faces downwardly rigid wages and prices will lose some degree of real flexibility if the nominal exchange rate is unable to adjust. Constraints on the adjustment of wages and prices in nominal terms should not, however, be confused with so-called real rigidities, which prevent real variables from returning to their equilibrium levels. The choice of monetary regime will not alter the economy's ability to adjust to shocks if real rigidities are present.

The mobility of labour and physical capital

A high degree of mobility in factors of production can be an effective substitute for changes in nominal exchange rates. Indeed, unlike the latter, which cannot bring about a permanent real adjustment in the face of asymmetric shocks, mobility of capital and labour is a route by which long-term adjustment can be achieved (see Mundell, 1961).

The dispersion in inflation, or more specifically expected inflation, rates

Large variations in expected inflation between countries would imply significant differences in short- and long-term real interest rates were those countries to be in a monetary union. This need not be a problem if, for instance, those differentials came about because poorer countries were 'catching up' with richer ones, e.g. via the so-called Balassa–Samuelson effect.[2] Inflation differentials may, however, reflect different cyclical positions, divergent labour market institutions, etc., which drive real interest rates away from their desired level.

The diversification of production

Countries with greater diversification in production should suffer a smaller macroeconomic impact in the face of idiosyncratic shocks to particular sectors. Thus, the need for terms of trade adjustments via the nominal exchange rate will be reduced, the more varied a country's output (see Kenen, 1969).

---

2 Prices in low-income countries may increase persistently faster than those in high-income nations. If poorer countries have faster productivity growth in their tradable sectors than rich countries, this would put upward pressure on wages in the tradable *and* non-tradable sectors in that country. Even if the prices of tradable goods are equalised over time, an inflation differential will remain because of faster growth of wages, and therefore prices, in the poor country's non-tradable sectors.

The similarity of economic shocks

With a 'one size fits all' monetary policy, the cost of joining a monetary union will partly depend on the severity of asymmetric shocks but also on the extent to which common shocks have an asymmetric impact on activity and employment. Greater commonality of economic shocks (or reactions to shocks) reduces the need for nominal exchange rate flexibility.[3] In addition, the more a group of countries satisfies this criterion, the less they need to satisfy other conditions, e.g. the flexibility of wages/prices or factor mobility.

The extent of economic openness

In countries highly open to international markets, domestic costs and prices are more likely to be affected by changes in the nominal exchange rate and fluctuations in international prices. Because the nominal exchange rate will have a smaller impact on the real exchange rate in the short term, it will be less useful as a macroeconomic stabilisation tool.

The extent of financial market integration

The greater the degree of financial market integration, the greater the opportunities for households and companies to smooth income shocks. Monetary union itself should foster deeper financial integration, increasing the opportunities for consumption smoothing in member countries. Deeper financial integration, however, may make it more likely that unsustainable financial imbalances will emerge between countries. In a world of imperfect capital markets, in which risks may be inaccurately priced, market interest rates may be pushed far away from their desirable level. To the extent that supervision and implicit support

---

3   Buiter (2000) makes the important point that the use of the nominal exchange rate to respond to shocks is potentially limited to demand shocks. Economic theory does not offer any concrete guidance on the desired response of the nominal exchange rate to aggregate supply shocks.

for banks remain national (as in EMU today), monetary union makes it more, not less, likely that a self-fulfilling loss of confidence in banks and sovereigns will take hold. Moreover, it increases the likelihood of destabilising financial contagion from 'periphery' to 'core' economies.

The degree of fiscal integration

Fiscal transfers by a supranational authority inside a monetary union should make it easier for member countries to adjust in the face of asymmetric demand shocks. This has been a standard argument in the optimal currency area literature since Kenen (1969). But for this argument to hold any weight, fiscal policy must be an effective stabilisation tool. In a Ricardian world without liquidity constraints, where consumers fully internalise the government's budget constraint, fiscal policy will be ineffective. In reality, though, the conditions for fiscal policy to be ineffective are very unlikely to be met. In the real world, a significant proportion of households will either be liquidity constrained or non-Ricardian in their behaviour. Moreover, that proportion is likely to be higher in exactly the kind of environment where fiscal transfers between member states are most needed to smooth economic shocks, e.g. in the aftermath of a financial crisis (see Corsetti et al., 2012).

The degree of political integration

For some authors, the political will to integrate is considered to be the most important factor that will determine the success of a monetary union. The extent to which other optimal currency area properties are satisfied *ex post* should be increased by a stronger desire for close political cooperation – institutional integration begets economic integration. If anything, however, the optimal currency area literature may have understated the need for deep political ties within a monetary union. Little attention was given to the nexus that exists between national banking systems and national governments and its potential to spawn financial dislocation within a monetary union. There is now almost universal agreement that it has to be severed if EMU is to survive.[4]

EMU as an optimal currency area in practice – fact or fiction?
The pro-EMU consensus

The previous section detailed the theoretical considerations that have been highlighted in the optimal currency area literature. This raises the question whether EMU satisfies those criteria. Even if the seventeen members do not constitute an optimal currency area, might the process of monetary integration itself create the conditions which help to sustain EMU in the future, the core argument in the endogenous optimal currency area literature? This seems to have been the broad conclusion of many authors in the years after the introduction of the euro.

There is a considerable body of work which tries to assess whether EMU is, or will become, an optimal currency area. This chapter will not attempt to review this literature – Mongelli (2008) is a useful starting point for that – but it will draw out its main conclusions. The widely cited *One market, one money* report into the costs and benefits of forming a monetary union in Europe, released by the European Commission in 1990, suggested the optimal currency area literature could not deliver clear policy guidance on this matter. In the subsequent twenty years, however, the balance of academic opinion has shifted in favour of monetary union in Europe. Earlier work on optimal currency areas was thought to overstate the costs of giving up monetary sovereignty and give too little emphasis to the benefits of a single currency. The 'endogeneity of optimal currency areas' gave further strength to this argument.

In the 'endogeneity of optimal currency area' paradigm, membership

---

4   This would include an EMU-wide deposit guarantee fund, direct bank recapitalisations via the European Stability Mechanism (ESM) and supranational supervision of financial institutions, potentially but not necessarily conducted by the ECB. Tentative steps towards a 'banking union' in Europe have recently been taken, but there remains considerable political opposition, particularly in Germany, towards some of these changes.

of a monetary union should not be judged on the basis that a country, or group of countries, satisfies specific criteria at the outset, but instead whether the necessary characteristics emerge out of membership of the monetary union (see Frankel and Rose, 1997). The main argument is that monetary integration leads to a deepening of reciprocal trade and more synchronised business cycles. But several authors have suggested that monetary integration can do more than just deepen trade linkages: it can further financial integration, reduce the asymmetry of shocks, foster policies which increase product and labour market flexibility, and increase political cooperation.

On balance, academic opinion has suggested that *ex post* tests will show that EMU is an optimal currency area. The closing remarks in Mongelli (2008) sum up that view: 'all in all ... the benefits [of EMU] outweigh the costs. There is greater resilience of the euro area as a whole, low actual and expected inflation, low interest rates and greater macroeconomic stability.' In light of recent developments, the consensus needs to be challenged critically.

Current account imbalances – sustainable or unsustainable?

Huge financial imbalances have emerged between member states. Although rising external surpluses/deficits in the 'core'/'periphery' economies can partly be explained by 'fundamentals', their scale and persistence suggest otherwise. Several authors previously suggested that the emergence of large external imbalances and the accompanying divergence of price competitiveness were sustainable equilibrium phenomena, driven by the 'Balassa–Samuelson effect'. Capital markets tell a different story – investors clearly do not believe that periphery debts are sustainable. This is not simply about the quantum of debt that has been built up; it is also about the accumulation of large external liabilities and the perceived inability of those countries to generate the external surpluses necessary to reduce those debt stocks over time inside a monetary union (see King, 2012).

Figure 4   **Euro zone countries' current account balances in 2007**
            % of GDP

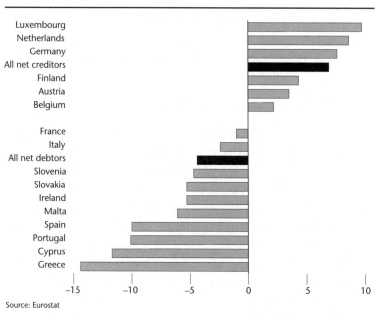

Source: Eurostat

In recent years, non-EMU countries have also built up large current account and net external debt positions – for example, the USA and Britain. The global driving forces behind these developments affected euro zone countries as well. What makes the problem so intractable for euro zone economies is the structure of EMU itself – a monetary union with fiscal policy determined nationally, an integrated financial market with national banking systems supported solely by host sovereigns, and a single labour market riddled with both nominal and real rigidities.

On the eve of the financial crisis, current account imbalances in the euro area ranged from –14 per cent to 8 per cent of GDP (see Figure 4). Greece, Spain and Portugal all ran current account deficits above 7 per cent of GDP on average in the five years before 2007. Germany, the Netherlands and Finland ran average surpluses in excess of 5 per cent of GDP over the same period. These averages are not dissimilar to the figures for the USA and China, the most conspicuous external debtor and creditor economies respectively. But whereas the US current account deficit peaked at 6 per cent of GDP in 2006, it did so at 15 per cent, 13 per cent and 10 per cent respectively for Greece, Portugal and Spain.

External debt and foreign asset positions

It is the dispersion of net foreign asset positions in the euro area, however – i.e. external stocks rather than flows – which is really striking. Despite sustained current account deficits in the USA over the last three decades, its *stock* of net external debt peaked only at 23 per cent of GDP (or $3.3 trillion) in 2008. This is only marginally larger than the equivalent figure for the euro area in aggregate. Cumulative current account deficits are far larger than this, suggesting sizeable valuation gains and beneficial currency moves. Meanwhile, China's stock of net foreign assets peaked at 34 per cent of GDP in 2007. Cumulative current account surpluses exceed the peak net foreign assets position, as might be expected for a country which has experienced a sustained upward move in its nominal exchange rate.

In 2007, three euro zone countries, Greece, Portugal and Spain, had net external debt in excess of 80 per cent of GDP. By 2009, Ireland could be added to that list. As a share of GDP, Italian net external debt was more limited, but it was still sizeable in cash terms. Between them, the five troubled euro zone economies had net external debts of roughly €2.5 trillion in 2010 (see Figure 4). Germany, the Netherlands and Belgium, the largest creditor nations in the euro area, had accumulated net foreign assets of €1.3 trillion (38 per cent of GDP), €0.2 trillion (29 per cent of GDP) and €0.4 trillion (77 per cent of GDP). Analysis of all OECD countries since the mid-1980s suggests these imbalances are extreme by past comparison: the inter-quartile range for OECD members' net foreign asset positions between 1985 and 2008 was −25 per cent to 10 per cent, according to Barnes et al. (2010a).

Figure 5   **Net foreign asset positions of selected countries in 2010**
% of GDP

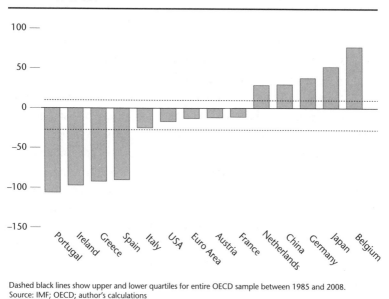

Dashed black lines show upper and lower quartiles for entire OECD sample between 1985 and 2008.
Source: IMF; OECD; author's calculations

Unsustainable external imbalances important in EMU – the role of the government and non-financial sectors

In theory, external imbalances need not be unsustainable. International saving and borrowing, as reflected in current account imbalances, is an important mechanism by which economies can adjust to economic shocks, share risk and accumulate wealth. Fundamental factors, such as demographics, risk preferences and future growth opportunities, may drive foreign borrowing and lending. It is entirely rational, for instance, for a relatively low-income country to borrow from abroad to finance productive investments in excess of domestic savings. Slower-growing, high-income economies with ageing societies may accumulate assets abroad as a way to fund future consumption.

Barnes et al. (2010b) confirm that these fundamental forces have played a role in fostering external imbalances within the euro area during the 2000s. The scale of the imbalances, however, cannot be fully explained by historical relationships. The unexplained component of the current account surpluses in Germany and the Netherlands, and the deficits in Spain, Portugal and Greece, are sizeable and 'noticeably larger than for earlier periods', according to the authors.

In Greece, and to a lesser extent Portugal, the main counterpart to the current account deficits and net external debt was excessive government borrowing. Both countries ran large and persistent budget deficits before the financial crisis, and amassed large stocks of government debt (see Figure 3). Much of this was financed by external borrowing – figures from the ECB suggest that less than 40 per cent of Greek and Portuguese government debt is owned domestically. Italy too has built up a large stock of public debt, and was running a budget deficit pre-crisis. But, as is also true of Belgium, which had amassed a stock of public debt equal to 84 per cent of GDP on the eve of the crisis, this largely reflects pre-1990 fiscal profligacy. Italy's overall budgetary position was unchanged before the financial crisis, with the government maintaining a primary surplus (general government net lending before interest payments) until the recession of 2008/09.

Spain and Ireland, by contrast, had very low levels of public sector net debt when the crisis struck. The Spanish and Irish governments both maintained primary surpluses for at least a decade before the crisis. Moreover, their overall budget balance actually improved in the period when their external positions deteriorated most rapidly. Instead, it was a dramatic increase in the non-financial private sector's investment relative to its savings which drove their current account deficits (see Figure 6). Net borrowing by households and non-financial companies in Spain and Ireland peaked at 14 per cent and 12 per cent of GDP respectively. In Ireland, it was driven mainly by households and an explosion in residential mortgage debt. By contrast, Spanish non-financial corporations were the primary driver of private sector borrowing, although by 2007 households were also running a financial deficit equal to 3 per

Figure 6 **Private non-financial sector's financial balance**
% of GDP

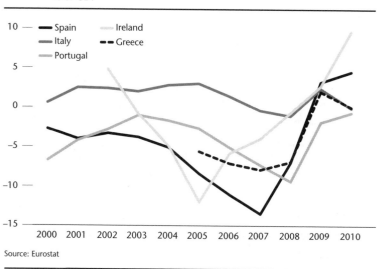

Source: Eurostat

cent of GDP. It is worth remarking that Portugal also saw heavy net borrowing by its non-financial private sector, dominated, as in Spain, by non-financial companies. The peak non-financial company financial deficit was a staggering 12 per cent of GDP (in 2008), compared with 11 per cent in Spain (in 2007) (see Figure 7).

The accumulated stocks of debt, which this borrowing led to, are even more telling. Portugal, Ireland, Spain and Italy all took on more private debt than the USA, supposedly the major 'borrower and spender' in the global economy.[5] The Greek private sector borrowed surprisingly little. One can add in general government net debt to get a figure for total non-financial debt in each economy.[6] For the USA, this figure

5   Gross debt of households and non-financial corporations does not include trade credit since this largely nets out at a sector level. Gross debt is calculated as the sum of each sector's borrowing in the form of loans and any securities (other than shares) which are outstanding.

6   To the extent that the general government is effectively one entity, it is reasonable to subtract the government's liquid asset holdings from its gross debt position.

Figure 7   **Non-financial companies' financial balance**
% of GDP

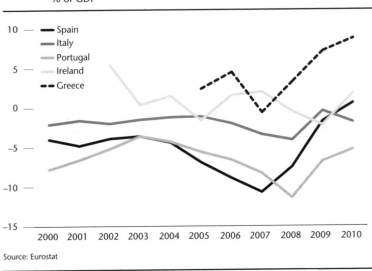

Source: Eurostat

reaches 215 per cent of GDP. In all five troubled euro area economies, total non-financial debt is larger than that of the USA (relative to GDP), most notably in Portugal, where it was three times national output when the crisis hit. By the end of last year, the gap between private debt (and total non-financial debt) in the USA and the euro zone periphery had got even larger (see Figure 8).

This brief survey of the data points to two developments that have been shared by the five troubled euro zone economies. Firstly, the build-up of historically large gross debt positions in the non-financial sector; and, secondly, sustained current account deficits, leading to sizeable stocks of net external debt for the economy overall. Fiscal profligacy has evidently not been common to all 'periphery' nations. Instead, it is the combination of a large non-financial sector debt burden and dependence on foreign borrowing which explains the predicament of troubled euro zone economies. It is notable, for instance, that France has yet to face the ire of markets despite having a stock of gross non-financial

Figure 8 **Stock of gross debt in domestic non-financial sector**
            % of GDP

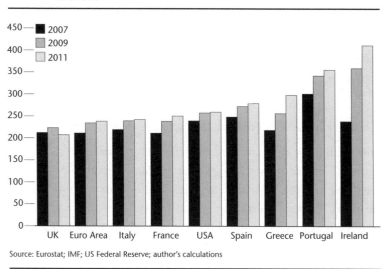

Source: Eurostat; IMF; US Federal Reserve; author's calculations

sector debt larger than that of the USA.[7] Although France's export performance over the last decade has been poor, its stock of net external debt was only 11 per cent of GDP in 2010. While gross debt positions cannot be entirely ignored, when it comes to the role of currency adjustments in response to economic shocks, it is changes in the net external debt position which are more important.

Nevertheless, the focus on net capital flows (mirrored by current account imbalances) and net foreign asset positions does not mean that we can ignore gross capital flows entirely. As Borio and Disyatat (2011) and Borio (2012) argue emphatically, the compression of risk premia globally cannot be explained with reference solely to net capital flows between countries, which primarily determine the underlying or equilibrium real 'risk-free' rate of interest. France may have run a persistent current account deficit before the crisis but it still provided large

7   French private non-financial sector debt and general government net debt were 160 per cent and 83 per cent of GDP at the end of 2010, according to Eurostat.

amounts of gross funding to periphery countries. Data from the Bank for International Settlements (BIS) show French-owned banks' claims on the five troubled euro zone economies amounting to $950 billion at their peak in 2008. German-owned banks' claims on these economies were, in fact, marginally lower on the eve of the crisis, despite the country being a large net creditor.

Capital flows were not used to finance productive investment

Any analysis of the euro zone crisis has to go farther than current account balances and net foreign asset positions in explaining the debt overhang in some EMU member states and the loss of confidence by investors. External imbalances within the euro zone may have been exaggerated by factors that had nothing to do with the structure of EMU itself. Even so, the fact remains that internal adjustment mechanisms within EMU did not prevent the emergence of unsustainable external positions between member states. Moreover, those mechanisms that are available do not appear sufficient to make the imbalances sustainable in the future.

Pre-crisis, the following argument was often heard: periphery countries with relatively low levels of real GDP per capita were catching up with richer north European economies. Greater growth opportunities and expectations of faster productivity growth justified elevated levels of fixed investment relative to the pool of domestic savings, hence the need for a current account deficit. Demand was likely to be high relative to supply capacity, pushing up inflation and depressing real interest rates. A rising real exchange rate would result. Rapid growth in private debt, net foreign liabilities and relative unit labour costs were all part of the adjustment to a new equilibrium. In this sense, the loss of price competitiveness in the 'periphery' is more apparent than real – productivity-enhancing investments today will help to reduce future unit labour cost growth as compared with foreign competitors.

The reality was somewhat different. Sustained current account

Figure 9   **Output per hour in manufacturing, average annual growth 1997–2007**
%

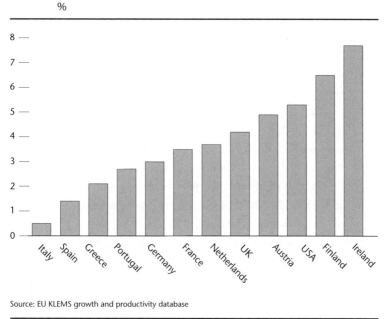

Source: EU KLEMS growth and productivity database

deficits were by and large not used to finance investment in productive assets. Greece and Portugal borrowed from abroad to finance excessive government spending. Spain and Ireland both witnessed remarkable construction booms, which have now imploded. Spain did have a relatively high rate of non-residential fixed investment; but sustained weakness in labour and total factor productivity growth, and returns on capital, does not suggest this has had a meaningful impact on supply capacity or corporate profitability (see Dannhauser, 2011). In fact, with the exception of Ireland, productivity growth across the periphery was feeble pre-crisis (see Figure 9).

Monetary policy does not have uniform effects even in a monetary union

Short-term and long-term nominal market interest rates were very similar across euro zone countries.[8] Expected inflation differentials would have led to some variation in *ex ante* real interest rates from the point of view of borrowers. Households or firms in periphery countries, for example, might have expected higher inflation and would therefore have perceived themselves as borrowing at lower real rates of interest. But what if monetary conditions, particularly the supply of bank credit, are determined by far more than just expectations of the future nominal short-term interest rates and inflation? What if the level of short-term interest rates itself affects risk-taking by banks? Are there not, in reality, powerful feedback loops between activity, asset prices and the money supply working through the balance sheets of borrowers and lenders (the so-called 'balance sheet' and 'bank-lending' channels) which might cause capital to be misallocated?

Monetary conditions were best conveyed by growth rates of broad money and bank credit, which show far greater variation between EMU members. While Germany saw average broad money growth of 4 per cent between 2002 and 2007, it grew by 12 per cent and 18 per cent in Spain and Ireland respectively. The suggestion that such differences can be ascribed to Balassa–Samuelson effects is far-fetched. Most obviously, the expansion of private credit in both Spain and Ireland centred on real estate and construction, where growth rates averaged in excess of 35 per cent in both countries in the run-up to the crisis. There was no evidence that either country was under-built at the start of the 2000s, or that this investment has boosted underlying productivity. Instead, rapid money and credit growth in Spain and Ireland went hand in hand with massive construction and property bubbles, which now threaten banking and government solvency.

---

8   To the extent that unsustainable imbalances were accumulating, this is clearly one of the adjustment mechanisms that failed to operate effectively before the crisis. Real long-term interest rates should have risen to reflect the increasing credit risk in periphery countries.

One important consideration in the formation of a monetary union is the similarity of responses to common shocks and the extent to which the single monetary stance is transmitted equally to member states. The view before the crisis was that euro zone countries showed considerable cyclical convergence and responded in a similar fashion to changes in euro area monetary policy. Business cycle asymmetries were deemed to be small and comparable with those of US regions, and the bulk of output fluctuations in euro zone economies were thought to arise from common shocks (see Giannone and Reichlin, 2006). The optimal currency area literature often glossed over variations in local legal systems, and the structure of domestic banking systems and financial markets. It turns out that such differences contributed to wildly different monetary conditions across euro zone countries. The transmission of ECB monetary policy and global liquidity trends did not simply vary between core and periphery; even within each grouping, there seem to have been vastly different reactions to common monetary shocks.

Membership of a monetary union exaggerated the accumulation of external debts and loss of price competitiveness. Suboptimal increases in countries' real exchange rates are particularly problematic given the loss of nominal exchange rate adjustment. The most extreme upswings in real exchange rates were witnessed in Greece, Spain and Italy before 2007.[9] The German real exchange rate declined by over 10 per cent between 1997 and 2007. Divergent unit labour cost trends explain most of the discrepancy in real exchange rates between EMU members. These in turn reflect a combination of faster growth in employee compensation and sluggish productivity growth in the tradable sectors of the periphery countries. The weakness of growth in manufacturing output per hour in Italy, Spain, Greece and Portugal is a particularly notable feature of

---

9   Throughout, real exchange rates are calculated on the basis of relative unit labour costs in manufacturing. Data are provided by the European Commission and are calculated on the basis of trade weights with all EU countries and nine additional major economies, the IC-36. Real exchange rate trends, encompassing more countries and based on relative CPIs, do not differ markedly.

Figure 10 **EU countries' export performance and cumulative real exchange rate moves, 1997–2007**

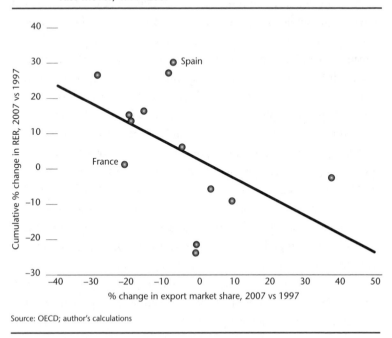

Source: OECD; author's calculations

the pre-crisis environment. It is worth noting as an exception, however, the extraordinarily strong productivity performance in Irish manufacturing. This might suggest that Ireland is better placed than the rest of the periphery to undertake the internal devaluation necessary to restore external balance in a monetary union. Indeed, with Irish manufacturing unit labour costs down by 35 per cent relative to trading partners since 2008, this process would seem to be well advanced.

The real exchange rate and relative labour costs are not, however, the only determinant of a country's ability to generate external surpluses over time. Export volumes will also be affected by geographical and product specialisation and a country's industrial structure will determine the extent to which domestic production can substitute for imports. Figure 10 shows the export performance of euro zone countries before the crisis.[10] Generally speaking, those countries that saw a faster rise in real exchange rates pre-crisis also saw a worse export performance. But there are some notable exceptions. France's share of its export markets dropped by 20 per cent in the decade before the crisis, despite a better-than-average performance in terms of relative unit labour costs. The loss of export market share by Spain, by contrast, was less than might have been feared given the 30 per cent increase in its real exchange rate between 1997 and 2007.

Do we need floating exchange rates to facilitate adjustments to economic forces?

Buiter (2000) argued that nominal exchange rate flexibility is not sufficient to bring about the kind of real adjustment now necessary in the periphery. Troubled economies will have to go through the pain of supply-side reform whether they are in a monetary union or not. This argument is theoretically compelling, but potentially open to criticism on empirical grounds. Nominal rigidities are what give monetary policy and movements in the nominal exchange rate real effects in the short run – if all expectations and prices immediately adjusted to a change in monetary policy, there would be no effect from a change in monetary policy. Buiter makes the point that real rigidities are, in fact, the constraint on economic performance over longer time horizons and this is, of course, true. But there is potentially an important asymmetry in nominal rigidities that makes the nominal exchange rate a more powerful stabilisation tool than he suggests.

It has long been known that nominal wages tend to be downwardly rigid. But, in a world where central banks target a low rate of inflation, internal devaluation may ultimately require outright declines in

---

10   This is the ratio of export volumes to import volumes in each country's export destinations, weighted by their share in exports; it is equivalent to each country's share in their export markets.

nominal wages. For the USA, at least, there is already evidence of significant resistance to nominal wage cuts and an increase in the share of workers affected by downward nominal rigidities (see Daly et al., 2012). Past work has not suggested any material difference in nominal rigidities between the USA and the euro zone. It should be noted that the impact of these nominal rigidities is the same regardless of the source of the need for adjustment within the euro zone. Even if the analysis above is not accepted, there is an undeniable need for adjustment and, in future decades, of course, different economic events might give rise to shocks that also require adjustment.

In today's unusual circumstances, a lack of nominal exchange rate flexibility may significantly extend the time frame over which real adjustment takes place, particularly given the labour and product market rigidities in EU countries. To some extent, labour mobility could help to offset this. The evidence, however, does not suggest that labour flows in the euro zone are particularly sensitive to economic conditions. Labour mobility within the euro area remains very limited by all accounts (see Zimmerman, 2009): relative to interstate and intra-state mobility in the USA, several studies have found it to be significantly lower. It is possible that the lack of labour movement arises because wages are sticky. For those who remain in employment, the absence of adjustments to real wages may be a disincentive to migrate. But it is likely that the constraints on intra-EMU labour flows have deeper roots. Language barriers are an obvious problem. Limited cross-border portability of social protection and pension rights is another. Given extensive regulation of professions across the euro zone, reciprocal recognition of qualifications has also been identified as a major constraint. Specific to this crisis, in Spain and Ireland in particular, is the problem of negative equity, which can inhibit labour mobility for owner-occupiers with an outstanding mortgage.

The Buiter critique may fail to hold in current circumstances for another reason. Normally, it is entirely reasonable to assume, as Buiter does, that the choice of exchange rate regime will have no significant, lasting impact on the path of potential output or the natural rate of unemployment. The long-run Phillips curve is vertical and the economy's long-run real equilibrium is determined by real factors alone. But, in the aftermath of the biggest financial crisis in a century, this is not obviously true. Hysteresis-type effects may well be important when activity is a long way below potential and the banking system is impaired as it is today. Faster demand growth in the short run may have permanent effects on an economy's supply capacity. The channels through which this might theoretically take place are numerous,[11] and have been discussed at length elsewhere. Their empirical relevance is an open question. The Great Depression is the only period of comparable economic stress, making econometric analysis all but impossible. Even then, the similarity is not perfect: in many ways, the recent crisis was more global in nature and even more threatening to the global financial system; moreover, economic activity in the second half of the 1930s was significantly boosted by rearmament in the run-up to World War II. To the extent that a country outside EMU retains nominal exchange rate flexibility, hence influence over the real exchange rate in the short term, it may, in today's unusual circumstances, be able to influence the level of real activity over the long term.

There is also a political dimension that should not be overlooked. If a country maintains influence over real exchange rates in the short run, or is able to allow changes in nominal and real exchange rates to respond to economic shocks, there will be a smaller upswing in unemployment and loss of output in response to shocks. It should then be less difficult for the government to build the electoral coalition necessary for supply-side reforms to remove the real rigidities that will restrict the level of real activity in the long run.

---

11 Including, for example, the deterioration of skills over the medium term, which makes it more difficult for those who are unemployed to find employment. As the period of unemployment lengthens, skills deteriorate further, and so on.

The British experience

In terms of the benefit granted by monetary independence, the comparison between the UK and troubled euro zone economies is notable. Households and businesses in Britain amassed a huge stock of debt before the financial crisis (see Figure 8). This was largely responsible for the bubble in residential and commercial property prices. Public sector debt has subsequently ballooned (to 71 per cent and 85 per cent of GDP at the end of 2011 for net and gross debt respectively, according to the IMF), in part because of the equity stakes taken by the UK government in two of the country's major banks. Yet, despite these structural frailties, Britain continues to enjoy 'safe-haven' status. At the time of writing, ten-year government bonds were yielding 2.1 per cent, a spread of only 15 and 55 basis points over US treasuries and German bunds respectively. Why might this be so? It could be because investors have greater confidence in the UK's ability to grow, and hence to service its debts, over the long term – the supply side of the economy, particularly the labour market, is deemed more flexible than elsewhere in Europe; the country's demographic prospects are also less gloomy. It is also possible that the government is perceived as more willing and able to implement the necessary fiscal consolidation and structural reforms. The UK's safe-haven status surely also rests, however, on the belief that monetary and currency flexibility provides the UK with the means to generate short-term output growth in the face of fiscal retrenchment, achieve the necessary rebalancing of the pattern of demand and production, and avoid the self-fulfilling losses of confidence that have historically plagued troubled economies inside fixed exchange rate systems.

Concluding remarks

Monetary union in Europe has ultimately been a political, rather than an economic, project. In fact, as Willem Buiter, now chief economist at Citibank, once put it: 'the whole European integration experiment ... has been a political wolf in economic sheep's clothing'. At the outset, there was general scepticism that EMU members constituted an optimal currency area. The balance of opinion before the financial crisis, however, was that EMU would develop the characteristics of an optimal currency area over time. Supporters of the 'endogenous optimal currency area hypothesis' seemed to win the day.

In light of recent events, this conclusion needs to be challenged. Even the strongest supporters of 'the European project' now accept the need for EMU's structure to be overhauled radically. If the euro zone is to evolve into an optimal currency area, it is going to need deeper political integration, including some form of fiscal burden-sharing and a banking union, involving supranational oversight and resolution of large financial institutions. The links between national governments and the banking systems they stand behind, which are ignored in the optimal currency area literature, have proved to be hugely relevant in the context of a monetary union. They are central to explaining the self-fulfilling losses of confidence we have witnessed across the euro zone's periphery. Deeper financial integration between EMU members has been a double-edged sword.

Limited labour mobility and the lack of a common fiscal policy were frequently cited as constraints on the effective operation of EMU. In hindsight, these have been less relevant than many authors had expected. It is highly unlikely that increased cross-border labour flows or larger fiscal transfers between EMU members would have prevented the accumulation of unsustainable financial imbalances. There was concern that, without nominal exchange rate flexibility, countries would not be able to adjust to country-specific shocks. In the end, it was not so much an asymmetry of shocks, but asymmetric reactions to common global shocks and a common monetary policy which were the euro zone's undoing. Distinctly national financial systems, inside a euro zone-wide financial market, help to explain why these divergences became so extreme.

Fundamental factors may explain some of the imbalances between member states; but their scale and persistence suggest that the euro area did not have sufficiently powerful *ex ante* adjustment mechanisms to prevent the emergence of unsustainable gross non-financial debt stocks in the periphery and net foreign asset positions across the euro zone. The dislocation in financial markets suggests that EMU, in its current form, does not have the *ex post* means for reducing those imbalances or debt levels either.

European leaders are in the process of redesigning EMU in order to cope with the current crisis and prevent the emergence of imbalances farther down the road. It is too early to tell whether they will be successful. Investors still believe that there is a risk of at least one country exiting EMU. This is not because EMU cannot be reformed in principle but, rather, because of the political constraints with which governments are faced. Disagreements about the future of Europe, which have shaped political and monetary integration over several decades, have not been resolved. And now a new threat is emerging. Periphery nations face a gruelling period of economic rebalancing. The cure for their ills is fiscal retrenchment and supply-side adjustment. It is far from clear, however, that we have the political leaders to sustain such reforms, or more importantly the electoral appetite to allow them to be sustained.

References

Altunbas, Y., L. Gambacorta and D. Marques-Ibanez (2010), 'Does monetary policy affect bank risk-taking?', BIS Working Paper 298.

Barnes, S., J. Lawson and A. Radziwill (2010a), 'Current account imbalances in the euro area: a comparative perspective', OECD Economics Department Working Paper no. 826.

Barnes, S., J. Lawson and A. Radziwill (2010b), 'Resolving and avoiding unsustainable imbalances in the euro area', OECD Economics Department Working Paper no. 827.

Bernanke, B. (2005), 'The global savings glut and the US current account deficit', Remarks at Sandridge Lecture, Virginia Association of Economists.

Borio, C. (2012), 'The financial cycle and macroeconomics: what have we learnt?', BIS Working Paper 395.

Borio, C. and P. Disyatat (2011), 'Global imbalances and the financial crisis: link or no link?', BIS Working Paper 346.

Borio, C. and H. Zhu (2008), 'Capital regulation, risk-taking and monetary policy: a missing link in the transmission mechanism?', BIS Working Paper 268.

Buiter, W. H. (2000), 'Optimal currency areas: why does the exchange rate regime matter?', Centre for Economic Performance Discussion Paper no. 462.

Corsetti, G., A. Meier and G. Müller (2012), 'What determines government spending multipliers?', IMF Working Paper 12/150.

Daly, M., B. Hobijn and B. Lucking (2012), 'Why has wage growth stayed strong?', Federal Reserve Bank of San Francisco Economic Letter 10/2012.

Dannhauser, J. (2011), 'Spain as the new Japan? Possible, maybe even likely', Monthly Review no. 269, Lombard Street Research.

Frankel, J. A. and A. K. Rose (1997), 'The endogeneity of the optimum currency area criteria', *Economic Journal*, 108(449): 1009–25.

Giannone, D. and L. Reichlin (2006), 'Trends and cycles in the euro area: how much heterogeneity and should we worry about it?', Working Paper Series 595, European Central Bank.

Kenen, P. (1969), 'The theory of optimum currency areas: an eclectic view', in R. A. Mundell and A. K. Swoboda (eds), *Monetary Problems in the International Economy*, Chicago, IL: University of Chicago Press.

King, M. (2012), Speech at the Lord Mayor's Banquet for Bankers and Merchants of the City of London at Mansion House.

Mongelli, F. P. (2002), 'New views on the optimum currency area theory: what is EMU telling us?', Working Paper Series 138, European Central Bank.

Mongelli, F. P. (2008), 'European economic and monetary integration, and the optimum currency area theory', European Economy

Economic Papers 302, Directorate General Economic and Monetary Affairs, European Commission.

Mundell, R. (1961), 'A theory of optimum currency areas', *American Economic Review*, 51(4): 657–65.

Tucker, P. (2012), 'National balance sheets and macro policy: lessons from the past', Speech at Society of Business Economists' annual dinner.

Viera, C. and I. Viera (2011), 'Assessing the endogeneity of OCA conditions in EMU', GEE Papers 0042, Gabinete de Estratégia e Estudos, Ministério da Economia e da Inovação, Portugal, revised November 2011.

Warnock, F. E. (2006), 'East Asian reserves accumulation and US interest rates', Testimony for 'China's financial system and monetary policies: the impact on US exchange rates, capital markets, and interest rates'.

Zimmerman, K. F. (2009), 'Labour mobility and the integration of European labour markets', Deutsches Institut für Wirtschaftsforschung Discussion Paper no. 862.

4 LESSONS FROM MONETARY HISTORY

John Chown

Introduction

Studying monetary history is particularly valuable in helping recognise and avoid bubbles, but it also puts one's prejudices and generalisations into perspective. Two, though, have stood the test of time:

- A long period of living with rigidly fixed exchange rates swings opinion in favour of the benefits of flexibility while, after living with floating rates, the public becomes nostalgic for the certainty of fixed rates.
- Whenever politicians and rulers interfere in monetary arrangements for political ends, disaster follows.

The first lesson of history is that before European Monetary Union (EMU) there were no examples of monetary union, between otherwise independent countries which have neither a federal central government nor a common fiscal policy, that have survived unless the countries concerned have gone on to become a fully fledged unitary or federal state. There are examples of monetary unions which ended in 'disunions'. This has included examples, as in the former Soviet Union, where previously sovereign states with a common currency broke up politically.

In the early days, economists pointed out the main technical problems of monetary union. It was hoped that the long-awaited 1995 European Commission Green Paper would address these problems and find a workable solution, but it turned out to be an entirely political, and economically illiterate, document which eventually resulted in the euro zone being launched in a form that ensured that it was a disaster waiting to happen.

There was no provision for dealing with the inevitable asymmetric shocks. What happens, for example, if one or more member countries have specific problems, or indeed opportunities, which require a realignment of relative cost structures or an adjustment of interest rate policies? The rules (which will have to be broken anyway) were intended (see Oborne and Weaver, 2011) to make devaluation and exit impossible. Such shocks are, in their nature, unpredictable, but sooner or later one would inevitably hit.

In fact, one longer-term problem was predictable and indeed predicted, but – as it happens – another problem in the form of the global financial crisis intervened before the demographic problems within the EU created the predicted tensions. The author's 2001 Chatham House paper 'Will the pensions time bomb blow apart European Monetary Union?' was, like the Eurostat paper on which it was based, intended not as a prediction but as a warning of a problem that would hit the EU by around 2020 on unchanged policies. Disappointingly, the warning has not been heeded and little has been done. This danger is still hanging over us – but another disaster has hit in the meantime. The politicians remain in charge; they are 'buying time' by throwing money at the problem while failing to address fundamental weaknesses of the present structure – including preparing for the pensions problem, which has not gone away. There is a huge political will behind the euro zone project which may be enough to carry the venture forward, at least for the next year or two. The precedents are not reassuring.

In the context of this early history of EMU, this chapter discusses the rise and fall of past monetary unions and the lessons to be learnt from previous attempts to introduce monetary union into the EU. After examining secondary and inflation-proof currencies and compromise proposals falling short of full monetary union, we look at how an understanding of history can influence what is happening today. Finally, we examine the problems of creating a fiscal union, drawing on the author's experience of international tax policy.

Past monetary unions and how they ended

Leaving aside those which eventually became full unions, other previous monetary unions all came to an end, and these have particular lessons for us. Many, like Latin Monetary Union discussed below, were little more than currency unions where countries adopting a gold or silver standard found it convenient to standardise the weights of the coins. Indeed, this was the nature of the US system at first as the US Constitution gives the federal government the sole right to coin money (see Chown, 2003). The Constitution made no mention of the then soon-to-be-developed banknotes and bank deposits. Monetary unions based on inconvertible fiat paper currencies are more relevant in terms of understanding EMU and they are discussed later in this section.

Latin Monetary Union

The Latin Monetary Union was based on a metallic rather than a fiat standard. It prospered, however, during the period when banknotes and bank deposits became an increasingly important component of the money supply and there was a huge growth in international trade and investment.

During the Napoleonic Wars, the UK left gold but maintained a stable currency, and after the war it restored the gold standard at the old parity. France, in contrast, had a disastrous experience with a paper currency and replaced it in 1803 with a new sound monetary system which it imposed on its occupied territories. After the wars, this system was adopted in some neighbours, and its success meant that the idea spread. The various Italian states had separate currencies but an increasing number of them adopted Latin Monetary Union standards, which were also followed when the country was united. The Swiss cantons had separate currencies but before they were united in 1850 they discussed whether they should adopt the French or the German system – until it was pointed out that the Germans still had three different systems after a succession of monetary unions (these were finally united only when Bismarck unified Germany as a nation).

Latin Monetary Union was a success, with the common currency greatly facilitating trade. It attracted some new members and its standards, at least for gold coins, were adopted unilaterally in several Latin American countries, Russia and elsewhere. There was a very interesting proposal in 1867 to transform the union into a world currency. John Kasson, in a supportive presentation to the US Congress on this issue, commented that 'the only interest in any nation that could possibly be injuriously affected by the establishment of this uniformity is that of the moneychangers – an interest which contributed little to the public welfare …' At that time, long before the invention of computers and online transfers, such costs were a fraction of those today. It was not to be: this was a 'simple technical solution beneath the dignity of politicians … more concerned with grand gestures and spin-doctoring than with solving practical problems for their citizens'. The British agonised about the trivial devaluation that would have been involved in trying to equalise the value of the different currencies (the UK delegate at the conference, Rivers-Wilson, playing the part of 'Sir Humphrey'); the French were concerned about the cost of minting and the loss of prestige.

The gold standard and the end of bimetallism

Originally, for accidental historical reasons, Latin Monetary Union was a bimetallic standard with the price of gold being 'fixed' at 15.5 times the price of silver. This caused problems, first when the market rates fell and silver coins disappeared into the melting pot! Towards the end of the century when the rates rose sharply, there was a disastrous unintended 'disunion' between the 'gold' countries (most of Europe and North America) and the 'silver' countries of India, the Far East and

Latin America. The serious consequences of this are discussed in Chown (2003).

In the UK, although officially on a silver standard since 1696, gold became the main circulating medium. A formal gold standard was introduced after the Napoleonic Wars. This worked well given the classic adjustment mechanism by which an adverse balance of payments simply caused an outflow of gold, reducing money supply and prices. Wages were flexible and the adjustment was usually fairly painless. This ceased to be true, however, in the interwar period, and the decision to restore the gold standard at the old parity proved disastrous. This is precisely the problem we are seeing in southern Europe today.

Another problem is that dependence on gold means that the narrow money supply can increase only as a result of the addition of newly mined gold. During the Industrial Revolution, though, the successive development of banknotes and bank deposits caused a substantial, and in the event more or less sufficient, increase in broad money supply. This is one of the arguments used against any restoration of the gold standard today.

The end of unions based on paper money

Austria-Hungary is the classic example of a monetary union not based on gold or silver. It was created in 1867 and the countries had independent fiscal policies, though a common defence and foreign policy. It is a complex story, but not a reassuring one for advocates of currency union. Austria had a turbulent history, both with regard to its politics and its monetary history. It had been continually using inconvertible paper money since 1762. An unsuccessful war with Prussia postponed the planned return to gold but, in 1867, Austria entered into a form of union with Hungary. Hungary was originally the junior partner but pursued sounder monetary policies and was more enthusiastic about a return to gold.

The union broke up after the 1914–18 war in a very messy way. In

October 1918, there was a revolution in Czechoslovakia, which became independent, and, after this, the joint monarchy quickly fragmented. Post-war trade sanctions applied only to Austria (which tried to maintain a monetary union with the successor states) and Hungary. Austria retained a bloated bureaucracy which was too expensive and there were the inevitable consequences. In January 1919, the Kingdom of the Serbs, Croats and Slovenes called in all Austro-Hungarian notes on their territory and over-stamped them, an example quickly followed by Czechoslovakia and, perforce, Austria in March. This was one of the first actions of the young Joseph Schumpeter, who had just been appointed minister of finance. He would have known what needed doing but soon resigned in frustration. Both Austria and Hungary soon took off into hyperinflation. Czechoslovakia came off the best, although at the cost of a sharp deflation. Poland, Romania and the Serbs, Croatians and Slovenes had a rough inflationary ride but avoided a disaster. The liquidation of the Austro-Hungarian Bank and the attempt to allocate its liabilities between the successor states is another tale of woe. It is to be hoped that the euro zone does not follow this approach.

When the Soviet Union ceased to exist at the beginning of 1992, all the fifteen successor states continued to use the rouble. The USA and the IMF actually thought this should continue (the EBRD, sensibly, disagreed). This is an extraordinarily complicated story but, inevitably, by 1994 all but one of the states had abandoned the rouble, usually bringing in an alternative 'coupon' currency. Inflation took off in a big way, and by 1994 prices in Russia had risen to 841 times the 1990 level and inflation was even higher in twelve out of the fourteen other republics. It is probable that none of them actually hit the classic '50 per cent per month' definition of hyperinflation, except perhaps for the odd month, although the excellent recent work on hyperinflations by Steve Hanke[1] does list them.

Yugoslavia had an even worse break-up. Old Yugoslavia (now

---

1   http://www.cato.org/publications/working-paper/world-hyperinflations.

Serbia) had two periods of hyperinflation, the second beating the previous 1947 Hungarian record. Of the other countries, Bosnia, Croatia and Macedonia fairly quickly established a more or less formal link with the Deutschmark/euro. Slovenia, the first of the countries to join the European Union, had no foreign exchange reserves and opted for a managed float on a crawling-peg basis. Montenegro, having won independence from Serbia, simply adopted the Deutschmark and then the euro as its actual currency.

Of the other former communist countries, the Baltic states were the first to declare independence. Estonia (see below) set up a very successful currency board with a link to the Deutschmark. Lithuania followed with a link to the US dollar, as did Latvia – though less successfully. On the whole, the other former communist countries were fairly successful in introducing a range of currency policies and have joined, or are hoping to join, the European Union.

In 1992, the Czech and Slovak republics decided to go their separate ways but originally intended to maintain a monetary union. The Slovaks, however, fearing that this would not last, transferred deposits to Czech banks and, to prevent capital flight, it was announced in October 1992 that the countries would enter into a currency union for at least the first six months of 1993. This was unconvincing and, in February 1993, Czechoslovak notes in Slovakia were called in and stamped. Citizens could convert 4,000 koruna in cash held on deposit and exchange controls were imposed. The Slovak currency initially traded at a discount of only around 10 per cent.

Precursors of EMU

There were two earlier attempts to approach monetary union in what was then the EEC, and James (2012) gives a very detailed account of the politics involved. All the issues which came up during the launch and again in the endgame of the euro zone were discussed at length in far more detail and with even more acrimony during these two periods.

Indeed, the need for a broader economic and fiscal union, with scope for inter-member transfers and for closer coordination of banking regulation, was regarded by the advocates of monetary union as essential and by others as unacceptable.

The Werner Report of October 1970 envisaged monetary union by 1980, involving either immutable parity exchange rates or a single currency. Liquidity, monetary policy with the outside world, public budgets and regional policy were all to be controlled at Community level, and capital markets were to be unified. This was a time when exchange controls were still widespread, and in a year when the international fixed rate regime collapsed in August!

Following the report, 'The Snake in the Tunnel' was set up in April 1972 by the six original EEC members, allowing for a maximum margin of fluctuation of 2.25 per cent between any pair of currencies. The United Kingdom joined for six weeks and other members went in and out. When the snake was finally ended (in 1978), the second stage of monetary union that had been intended to begin in 1974 was postponed indefinitely.

The next initiative was the Delors Report in April 1989. Monetary union was to be based on fixed exchange rates with a single monetary policy conducted by a European system of central banks. Germany, the UK and Luxembourg wanted to move forward gradually, but the enthusiasts, France, Italy and Spain, feared that without institutional changes their countries might not be able politically to get their inflation rates and performance under control. Many people thought monetary union would never happen. Odd as it now seems, although it was rightly said that capital movements must be fully liberalised, a common currency was not seen as an essential feature of monetary union, but might be a natural development.

Although the report was widely expected to be dropped, as Harold James explains, Delors, in the best *énarques* tradition, had manipulated opinion so that not only did he achieve the creation of the Exchange Rate Mechanism, he sowed the seeds for the future introduction of EMU. A major debate in the early 1980s was whether this required, or was even inconsistent with, free movement of capital.

As with the Snake, there were very many devaluations, realignments and other adjustments and, of course, the other major currencies (for example, the dollar and the yen) were fluctuating widely. For the first five years until 1984, exchange rates and inflation differentials converged and all seemed well. It did not last, however. Again, there was no real convergence.

One issue which was perhaps to be decisive was the reunification of Germany, where, to the astonishment of economists, the introduction of the Deutschmark into East Germany was created without preparation, without economic adjustment and at the wrong exchange rate. This disastrously destroyed the competitive position of East Germany. The governor of the German central bank, Pohl, said that monetary union in Germany was a 'political decision'. In the following year, Pohl, citing this experience, warned the European Parliament against the premature introduction of monetary union.

Margaret Thatcher and her economists had been opposed to monetary union. They preferred to use interest rates to stabilise the price level rather than the exchange rate. Robin Leigh Pemberton, the governor of the Bank of England, however, liked the idea of having an anchor to bring down inflation rates. Astonishingly, just five days after German reunification, the UK actually joined the Exchange Rate Mechanism. The chosen central rate of DM2.95 also seems to have been another 'political decision'. Everything worked – for a time – and John Major unexpectedly won the April 1992 election, but the UK exited on 16 September 1992, described – perhaps inappropriately – as 'Black Wednesday'.

There are two lessons from this history. The first is a common problem: where a currency is perceived to be out of line, throwing money at it is generally money wasted. The second lesson is positive, and certainly confirmed that currency rate adjustment, coupled with appropriate monetary policy, can lead to a substantial recovery and a prosperous outcome. The whole episode, though, was a political disaster.

Secondary and inflation-proof currencies

It has often been suggested that a secondary currency, operating along-side national currencies, could achieve many of the benefits (and fewer of the problems) of a full monetary union. Many such proposals go farther and suggest we should try to create a currency which is a more reliable store of value than existing fiat currencies. These are both excellent ideas and the two different concepts are not, in principle, mutually exclusive. The hard ecu proposal, which was made during the monetary union debate, was intended to achieve both, but as discussed below, previous attempts to do this have achieved neither. The precedents for an inflation-proof currency are not encouraging, but there was far more scope for an inflation-proof secondary currency approach.

An inflation-proofed currency?

There is a long history of attempts to introduce a sound inflation-proof currency but none has really worked. In 1887, Alfred Marshall had suggested that gold was no longer a stable measure of value, and that we should examine using 'a tabular standard of value' (i.e. a price index which would constitute an optional unit of account for long-term commitments). There have since been many attempts, usually unconnected with monetary union, at creating a stable currency. Germany, in the aftermath of inflation, experimented with the Rentenmark, backed by mortgages, and discussed a 'Roggenmark' backed by rye. 'Monetary Correction' was used (for a time successfully) in Brazil and, of course, inflation-indexed bonds have been issued in many countries, including the UK. There is no convincing historical precedent for a successful inflation-proofed currency, although in more stable times gold or silver may have served this purpose. Bretton Woods was partly successful for a time.

The 'All Saints Day Manifesto' of 1975 published in *The Economist* suggested the introduction of an inflation-proofed 'Europa' as a secondary and alternative currency which could in due course become the currency of Europe. Its value would be a weighted average of the participating currencies adjusted by movements in the consumer price indices. This looked very appealing but *The Economist*, in its editorial comment, was more sceptical, describing it as 'indexed-linked securities (called money) not under the control of national governments': sensibly, they wanted monetary union to evolve naturally in the marketplace without official edicts and legalistic structures.

This idea was taken up by others and, in 1990, John Major announced his support for the 'hard ecu' proposal in a document entitled *The Next Stage in an Evolutionary Approach to Monetary Union* by Sir Michael Butler and Paul Richards. The formula was intended to ensure that this secondary currency would be as strong as the strongest currency in the region. I was not then, and am not now, convinced that the formula suggested in either case would actually produce the result intended.

Saving transactions costs

There was far more scope for using a secondary currency to try to reduce transactions costs. Chown and Wood (1989) proposed that the 'right road to monetary union' was to introduce into circulation immediately a 'basket ecu', a concept which already existed as the weighted average of the various relevant currencies. As and when this became established, travellers within the EU would have to carry only one 'foreign' currency with them while shopkeepers, hotels and other suppliers of services would not have to cope with a wide range of currencies, but would simply double-price in their local currency and ecus. This would substantially reduce transactions costs, which, in turn, would encourage more travellers and businesses to use the new system. It would also make it easier to compare prices across frontiers as these became expressed in ecus, thus enhancing competition. The starting point in Chown and

Wood was, of course, that any change should be designed to benefit the citizen, as traveller, trader and investor, rather than to be part of a power play designed to make life easier and tidier for governments.

The most often cited benefit of EMU was that foreign exchange losses and costs would be reduced or eliminated. We analysed this, and showed that about three-quarters of what business records as 'foreign exchange losses' mainly arise, not from currency fluctuations (which might typically average out over time), but from bank charges and commissions. These charges were, at the end of the twentieth century and in spite of the development of electronic techniques, significantly higher than they had been a century and a half earlier when Latin Monetary Union was being proposed. The European Commission could have reduced these by a positive use of competition policy; in practice, for whatever reason, they always backed away from any serious initiative. Big businesses can look after themselves but the prevailing situation is such that the euro has left a lot of smaller businesses without the promised transactions costs advantages, and this calls into question whether the cost aspect (the real alleged benefit for business and travellers) had really been addressed by the political enthusiasts for monetary union, or whether they had a quite different agenda.

Other compromise solutions

Given that it is probably impossible to create a full and rigid monetary union in the absence of a greater degree of fiscal coordination than can be achieved democratically within present institutions, it would have been better to have found a second-best solution with fewer long-term side effects. There are various such second-best solutions.

Shadowing and 'fixes'

Formal monetary unions apart, there are many compromises between fixed and floating rates. There are many examples where a country simply shadows another's currency, but where there is no technical problem in terminating the arrangement. This was followed successfully in South-East Asia, and countries such as Bulgaria and Bosnia have been shadowing the euro. Because their shadowing was not entirely credible in the eyes of the markets, that arrangement did not lead to the bubble-creating investment from which Greece and other periphery countries suffered (see the chapter by Dannhauser) – risk premia were not entirely eliminated. There are also other compromise variations such as crawling pegs and inflation targeting, but these are not immediately relevant to us.

Many countries in South-East Asia had been formally or informally shadowing the dollar, and the more foolish speculators were picking up a nice interest rate profit in uncovered investments in Asia. This led to profits until the Thai baht devalued in 1997, followed by others. The problem here was that the inflow of funds stimulated an artificial price bubble. Bangkok was littered with half-finished building projects. After devaluation and an IMF rescue, most of them, but not at first Indonesia, made a good recovery.

A year later, in 1998, the banks lost even more by riding the extraordinary interest rates on Russian GKOs (treasury bills) in what they thought was a stable currency pegged to the dollar. Russian treasury bill rates had been about 50 per cent, reflecting the then rate of inflation. Inflation fell very sharply but nominal interest rates did not, so there was a real rate of over 30 per cent, which could, it was thought, be locked in by hedging the dollar/rouble exchange rate. The banks worked out how much they would make on this deal over a year: we calculated that they would bankrupt the government within eight months. The government defaulted and the exchange rate devalued against the dollar.

Turkey had long suffered chronic inflation at rates above 50 per cent per annum. The collapse of the currency against the dollar was checked by an IMF stabilisation package in November 1999 coupled with a credible 'crawling peg' exchange rate policy. Purchasing power parity held during this period against the US dollar, which the IMF thought was the obvious target. Unfortunately, this was a period when the euro zone currencies fell sharply against the dollar and Turkey's competitiveness against its main trading partners deteriorated by over 30 per cent. There was the inevitable crisis in early 2001 and, after the central bank had fallen into a classic trap and wasted $10 billion in support operations, the currency was floated in February. As so often happens, things have to get worse before they get better and, in this case, a new government succeeded in getting expenditure under control, granting independence to the central bank and liberalising the economy. This initiated a period of prosperity from which they have not so far looked back.

Bretton Woods

In the negotiations leading up to Bretton Woods, Keynes had argued, unsuccessfully, that the burden of any adjustment process could be shared equally by creditor and debtor countries. The approach involved initially fixed exchange rates against the dollar (until 1971 itself fixed in terms of gold), bolstered by international transfers negotiated by the IMF but with the right, and indeed the obligation, to change the rate when there was a 'fundamental disequilibrium'. This happened very often (as the excellent Pick's *Currency Year Book* regularly listed) but at least there was a provision for adjustment. The original design of EMU should have included such a workable proposal for exit.

Bretton Woods in its heyday was, in theory at least, a gold exchange standard: the US dollar fixed at $35 per ounce was the anchor currency for the rest of the world, which at first suffered from a 'dollar shortage', a term which actively persisted even after the dollar itself became a weak currency, at least against Germany and Japan. Indeed, after the Vietnam-induced inflation, Nixon broke the link in 1971 and this was the beginning of the end of Bretton Woods.

The sterling area

The sterling area, being informal, worked well for many years, but because it was informal it fell apart when it became less relevant. The only monetary authority was the Bank of England. Other countries had no say in UK monetary policy nor, after they ceased to be colonies, any obligation to follow it. In the area's heyday, however, they had strong incentives to remain in the club, one of the benefits of which was freedom from exchange control (within the area). Some early leavers, such as New Zealand, introduced their own currency without any immediate or expected change in parity. Others (Nigeria and the Caribbean countries), which mostly had had currency boards, also eventually opted out, as discussed (see below).

Could such an approach have been applied in the euro zone? The same result could have been achieved economically, but certainly not politically, if countries had accepted Germany's Bundesbank as the monetary authority and voluntarily adopted their currency. This is effectively what, for example, Estonia did very successfully. Note issues and the monetary base were the responsibility of the central bank or currency board of the country concerned, which would then be free to pursue an independent monetary policy having regard to reconciling internal with external balances.

This would not necessarily have helped Ireland in the current crisis as a solvent and well-managed country faced with a housing bubble aided and abetted by a banking system that was too large for the country. The Irish needed, and knew they needed, high interest rates to deal with this, but this would not have been possible while remaining within a 'Deutschmark area'. The fatal mistake which Ireland made was the unnecessarily generous bailout of the banking system (see Carswell, 2011). Larger states, such as Italy and Spain, had similar – but in some respects different – problems (again, see the chapter by Dannhauser). Iceland was rather more complex, with an enormous, unsound, banking system which could never have been underwritten by the state. Not being part of the euro zone, however, it could and did devalue and default and has made a good recovery.

Currency boards

A currency board issues notes redeemable at a fixed rate of exchange with a reference currency such as sterling, dollars or the euro. Redemption is backed, usually 100 per cent, by interest-bearing treasury bills in that currency. Provided this guarantee is honoured on outstanding notes, however, the country is free to adopt a new replacement currency at any time. These days, notes are only a small proportion of the money supply and a currency board is credible only if banks are required to hold their reserve assets in notes of, or deposits with, the currency board. During the Asian crisis, some had thought that Hong Kong might be affected, but their very sound currency board ensured that the rate was held. There could have been pressure on the banking system but, given that their reserve base was sound, there was not.

Estonia is a particularly interesting case of a currency board inside the EU. In June 1992, it abandoned the rouble to create its own currency, with Eesti Pank acting in effect as a currency board required to hold 100 per cent of the monetary base in foreign assets. The exchange rate was thus credibly fixed at eight kroon to the Deutschmark, adjusted in due course to the euro. The switch from a distrusted currency to a solid link with a sound one caused a substantial one-off adjustment in the price level. This, as we now understand, is inevitable, but a one-off change is not to be confused with inflation, which is best described as a chronic tendency for prices to rise. The currency was linked to the Deutschmark at a rate far below purchasing power parity and, once the exchange rate was accepted as sustainable, this could be corrected only by higher prices. Prices rose by 46 per cent during the two months after the change and doubled over the next two years. To keep real interest rates in line, nominal rates had to remain high, but few seem to have taken advantage of the apparent arbitrage opportunities because of a distrust of the banks (Eesti Pank, of course, could offer only a margin less than the Deutschmark rate, as its assets were, by definition, in Deutschmark securities).

Former British Caribbean colonies originally retained their currency board link to sterling but, either when sterling was devalued in 1967 or when it was floated in 1972 and exchange control was imposed on the outer sterling area, they changed without fuss to a link with the US dollar. The Barbados Board is now required to hold only the equivalent of 60 per cent of its liabilities in US dollar assets but, in practice, often has more.

A currency board is potentially a highly disciplined way for a country to fix its currency to that of another country. The country, though, loses its right to 'solve' its financial problems by printing money, but does earn seigniorage at the rate of interest available on treasury bills issued by the country being shadowed. The country still has, and indeed needs, control of the supply of bank money.

An alternative is 'dollarisation', where a foreign currency is simply used as the national currency. In our context, this is really a form of secondary currency discussed above (with, say, the dollar being used through choice within the country concerned either as the only currency or as a secondary currency). This approach transfers the seigniorage profits to the country issuing the adopted currency, however, and leaves the dollarised country with even less ability to deal with monetary policy.

One suggestion seriously made in the early post-communist days was that the most cost-effective way of helping Russia was to ship out US dollar bills, which could be paid out by the government to meet their expenditure. These then would be put into circulation in Russia (where the dollar was already in frequent and, at first, illegal use) as a secondary currency. In practice, though, this would not have worked as, at that time, the outflow of oligarch funds from Russia was more or less equal to the level of international aid.

Either a currency board or the adoption of the Deutschmark in a process equivalent to 'dollarisation' could have been used by any country – or group of countries – to gain the transactions costs benefits of a single currency without creating the euro and using it as the only currency across a large part of the EU.

General conclusion – and the future?

History confirms that no previous monetary union has survived unless it was the precursor of a genuine union of nations. Survival of any shared monetary arrangements has three prerequisites:

- Effective arrangements for ensuring that each country maintains fiscal discipline.
- Absolutely clear provisions that (as with long-standing and fully fledged federal unions) each state is responsible for its own debts.
- Adequate arrangements for emergency interstate transfers – with IMF-type safeguards and conditions – as happened in the days of the Bretton Woods system.

Other chapters examine these issues, but an analysis of history leads me to a pessimistic conclusion.

A well-managed fiscal union with a proper constitution might provide the backdrop for a lasting monetary union without full political union. This would still be difficult to achieve, however. Member states would have to make regular adjustments to taxes and expenditure to keep their budgets in balance, using fiscal policy and reforming labour laws to keep wage rates competitive.

At the start of the crisis, I took the view (though without making the very detailed calculations that I hoped, perhaps optimistically, the ECB and the European Commission would have been making) that Greece should have been allowed or required to leave the euro zone, float its currency and enter into an organised default. It could then have been helped by conditional financial assistance directed at reforming the economy. There would have been significant costs involved in recapitalising the banks and in taking measures to deal with the inevitable contagion. Delaying action, however, is much more expensive.

The authorities are saying they will pay 'whatever it costs' to save the euro zone – but from where will the money come? The Commission budget is tiny so there are only two options. Either Germany pays (the other non-crisis countries being much smaller) or monetary policy will be used, which risks inflation and therefore will be blocked by Germany. The whole question of whether fiscal union will be acceptable to even the inner group of countries needs to be addressed (see below).

The present policy relies on 'internal devaluation', which involves deflation and government budget adjustments in the weaker countries. One does not have to be a Keynesian to believe that this could create a generation-long recession which would itself slow down the repayment of debts, and that devaluation and default would bring about quicker adjustment. In the event, several, but not all, of the weaker countries have managed better than we had expected in rationalising their labour markets and getting costs and budgets under control. It could all work, but the lessons of history are not promising. We therefore have to look at the alternatives, hoping that there is a Plan B that is carefully thought through (including those suggested in other chapters) rather than a chaotic collapse.

One outcome might then be for a core of countries, led by Germany, to retain a common currency and agree to coordinate a broader economic policy, with or without the need for a more formal fiscal (or even federal) union. Outer euro zone members, having devalued or floated and probably also partly defaulted, would have their own currencies.[2] If the new currencies, initially or eventually, had a new credible and sustainable fixed rate of exchange with the euro they might then choose to rejoin.

Citizens and traders could be permitted, and indeed should be actively encouraged, to contract and generally conduct their business in 'new euros', which may, in the course of time, become the preferred currency, effectively superseding the local currency.[3] This would in effect amount to the countries (or their citizens) choosing to adopt a

---

2   At first, these could be over-stamped euros.

3   This is essentially the idea floated by Geoffrey Wood and myself in our 1989 IEA paper *The Right Road to Monetary Union*. Pedro Schwartz has also proposed that a country such as Greece should be allowed to introduce its own currency while encouraging the use of the euro as a parallel currency with neither being formal legal tender.

German-dominated currency as their own. It would be less formal than membership of the euro zone or a currency board. Market forces, rather than political scheming, could well lead towards a full monetary union, with everything happening in a logical order.

This would still leave the complex question of how the inner group could move forward without imposing its rules on (or being blocked by) the departing members plus the UK, Sweden and Denmark, with the present applicant members having to choose which way to go. The UK in particular will have to use superb diplomacy, with first-class monetary economic advice, in the negotiations, and must not risk breaking up the European Union as such.

A fiscal union? Tax and pensions aspects

No monetary union has, so far, lasted without becoming something distinctly more federal. As such, the question of whether a fiscal union is appropriate does need to be addressed. Federal unions can still leave a substantial measure of independence to states. The present solution, if it is to work, will require euro zone members to move towards a fiscal union which may, in turn, involve a transfer union or a euro zone system of bank guarantees. Would the proposal stand up to a full analysis of the consequences by the various members?

It has been argued that one cannot have monetary union without something approaching a common tax system. This is the reverse of the truth. The only economic weapon left to member states for dealing with asymmetric shocks would then be on the government expenditure side. It has been clear that various attempts by the EU to move towards what they call 'tax harmonisation' are really aimed at 'standardisation'. They have refused to discuss proposals to solve some very real problems of cross-border investment because of this emphasis.[4]

---

4   See John Chown, 'Eliminating tax obstacles for cross-border operations', at the conference 'Recent developments in European company law' (206D21), Academy of European Law, Trier, 16 February 2007.

Even if there is no central guarantee of member states' debts, there would presumably have to be both some central control of national budgets and provisions for interstate transfers, which could, in certain circumstances, become substantial. Any country considering signing up for such a union would be well advised to compare its properly calculated balance sheet as a nation with those of the intended partners with even more thoroughness than companies contemplating a merger. Apart from looking at the formal debts, projected budgetary cash flows and other figures which should be readily available to the enquirer, they should look at other ways in which the nation's solvency can be seriously affected. This will determine whether it will have to contribute to, or be able to make claims upon, the group as a whole. One of the key issues here is pensions, which are discussed below. There are other issues involved in drawing up such a balance sheet such as public–private partnerships and the remaining scope for privatisation. Help to member states with problems should be carefully designed to ease the transition rather than to postpone action.

In the USA, the individual states have their own credit ratings, even though the country is far better placed to act as a union than the EU given the common language and a much higher degree of labour mobility than Europe. Switzerland is a rare example of a multilingual federation – but will those pressing for an ever-closer union welcome the degree of taxing rights enjoyed by Swiss cantons and communes?[5] The Australians have complex arrangements for leaving their states with a degree of control over some taxes and expenditure, calculating the federal contribution on perceived standard needs rather than on actual expenditure. Brazil, also a federal country, has had problems keeping the financing of its states under control.

As with the Bretton Woods system and the IMF, steps would have

---

5   Instead of political parties competing to bribe voters for their money, cantons compete to attract people and business, keeping tax rates sensible. Some forms of social payments are handled at the level of the communes, which, it is said, ensures efficient monitoring – people realise that neighbours who are cheating the system are cheating them.

to be taken from time to time to bail out problems, even though, as suggested above, it would be essential to ensure that the market understood that it was possible for member states to default just as US states, and Stockton in California, have done.

One big issue is the problem of ageing populations.[6] This has very different consequences for different EU members, on which the author has been publishing analysis for over a decade. British and French citizens have very similar expectations of earnings-related pensions, but while the British ones are backed by some $2 trillion (about 80 per cent of GDP) of assets in independent funds, in France these are an 'off-balance-sheet' liability of the state. The updated Eurostat[7] figures show that on unchanged policies, by 2060 the French government will be paying out 16.8 per cent of GDP to pensioners every year – double the UK figure of 8.4 per cent. Indeed, policies have changed for the worse. One of the first actions of Hollande was to reverse the modest increase in the pension age introduced by his predecessor. This is why the author warned in a paper to Chatham House in 2001 against any UK involvement with reforms that might lead to a raid on these funds.

The UK is not, and obviously will not be, a member of the euro zone, but most of those countries that are, including Germany, have 'Bismarckian' rather than funded pension arrangements, like those in France. Even for those countries, the detailed differences in obligations are very different. If two companies were merging we would examine the detailed long-term assets and liabilities of both. Countries should do the same if there is to be a fiscal union. Will the German taxpayer, for instance, be prepared to subsidise early retirement for the French?

What of other countries? The Netherlands and Finland would surely both be part of the inner group. They have over 100 per cent and 60 per cent of GDP respectively in pension funds and should watch this

---

6   This was discussed in the author's 2001 Chatham House paper 'Will the pensions time bomb blow apart European Monetary Union?'

7   See the 2009 Eurostat Ageing Report: http://ec.europa.eu/economy_finance/ publications/publication_summary14911_en.htm.

situation very carefully indeed. Denmark has a high level of privately funded pensions. Sweden does not, but has taken steps to 'de-risk' its state pension system.

Thus, we can see that a fiscal union would not be a trivial step. Euro zone member states should not simply allow themselves to evolve into a fiscal union by default. Fiscal union should not be thought a mere technical step which, once followed, can lead to a sustainable monetary union. It is a matter that should be given the same serious consideration as the price paid in a merger of two large conglomerate companies. The euro zone was formed as an experiment in monetary union without historical precedent. History also suggests that there is no easy solution to the crisis.

References

Carswell, S. (2011), *Anglo Republic: Inside the bank that broke Ireland*, Penguin Ireland.

Chown, J. (2003), *A History of Monetary Unions*, New York: Routledge.

Chown, J. and G. E. Wood (1989), *The Right Road to Monetary Union*, Inquiry 11, London: Institute of Economic Affairs.

James, H. (2012), *Making the European Union*, Cambridge, MA: Harvard University Press.

Oborne, P. and F. Weaver (2011), *Guilty Men*, London: Centre for Policy Studies.

5 BETTER OFF IN?

Andrew Lilico

In this chapter, five interrelated issues will be considered.

- To what extent, if at all, issues of balance of payments 'imbalances' within the euro zone are really distinct from issues of indebtedness, high deficits and competitiveness.
- The extent to which competitiveness differentials are sustainable within a currency union as opposed to requiring either significant 'internal devaluation' or currency break-up in order for the problems to be addressed.
- The relative merits of internal and external devaluation as tools for addressing competitiveness issues and making capital flows sustainable.
- The past experience of key euro zone member states in cutting deficits without significant offsetting currency depreciation.
- The forms of fiscal transfers that might and might not offset market-driven internal capital flows within the euro currency union in order to make it more stable.

Are balance of payments 'imbalances' an issue in themselves, or are they symptoms of other issues?

Many commentators contend that there are significant issues within the euro zone relating to balance of payments problems. They argue that there is a structural current account surplus for Germany and a near-matching current account deficit for the indebted countries such as Portugal, Italy, Spain and Greece, and that this is a problem of itself. A strong case can be made, however, that the balance of payments issues are not a separate problem of their own, but a symptom of other issues – sometimes good; sometimes bad. It is a mistake to believe, as some propose, that there should be international mechanisms to prevent the build-up of payments imbalances. Doing so could prevent perfectly healthy imbalances arising.

There are three main elements to the balance of payments issue:

- When the government budget deficit is higher in one country than in another, that tends to lead to a capital account surplus (as foreign capital is sucked in to fund the budget deficit) and thus to a current account deficit. Hence reducing government budget deficits will tend, fairly automatically, to reduce current account deficits.[1]
- When one country has a higher growth rate than another in a process of GDP convergence, investment opportunities may be more attractive in the high-growth country, sucking in capital and leading to a capital account surplus and hence a current account deficit. So, when Greece (for example) was growing more rapidly than Germany in the 2000s, it was natural that Greece should attract German capital and hence run a current account deficit relative to Germany. But, if Greece grows more slowly than Germany over the next decade, there will not be capital inflows from Germany (fiscal transfers aside, which we shall explore below) and hence there will not be the same current account deficit. Hence slower growth in indebted countries, relative to Germany, over the next decade will tend to reduce current account deficits.[2]

---

1   This may put some readers in mind of the 'New Cambridge' hypothesis of the 1970s, though my position, unlike the New Cambridge one, is orthodox.

2   It will also be the case that there may be natural capital flows when a country's sustainable growth rate rises relative to another's, even if the first country's is lower. For example, suppose capital flows are in equilibrium and there are two economies, A and B, with A growing sustainably at 2 per cent per year and B growing at 4 per cent. If A's sustainable growth rate rises to 3 per cent and B's stays at 4 per cent there will naturally be capital flow from B into A. This effect could have been a factor in the large capital account surpluses the USA experienced in the 1990s, even with higher-growth economies; a rise in the

- The above two points indicate natural factors that can drive current account deficits. But capital inflows were probably also associated with an unsustainable build-up of debt, as evidenced by the competitiveness differentials, as we shall see below.

Thus, balance of payments issues are (i) a symptom of the budget deficit, competitiveness and debt issues; and (ii) insofar as they are not automatically addressed when addressing budget deficits, competitiveness and household indebtedness, are often healthy and natural. On the other hand, even if payments imbalances arose naturally, that does not necessarily mean that they did not presage future risks. For example, capital flows from Germany to Greece could have been based on mistaken assumptions about the relative future growths and stabilities of Germany and Greece.

To what extent are competitiveness differentials sustainable within a currency union?

While some capital flows, during the 2000s, from Germany into Greece and other now-distressed parts of the euro zone could be justified by more rapid Greek growth, it also now seems certain that some of that more rapid Greek growth was itself a consequence of a build-up of debt supported by capital inflows. One standard way to think about the question of how much of the capital inflows might have reflected sustainable economic forces and how much might have reflected unsustainable debt build-up is to analyse trends in competitiveness.

When discussing competitiveness differentials within the euro zone, it is common to consider trends in relative unit labour costs. Consider Figure 11. This figure considers how real unit labour costs have evolved

---

underlying growth rate of the USA might have justified capital inflow even from higher-growth countries. Capital flows can also occur, of course, owing to differences in savings rates in different countries. Again, we would expect these to be self-correcting in the long run.

Figure 11 **Real unit labour cost trends, 1999–2011, selected euro members**
1999 = 100

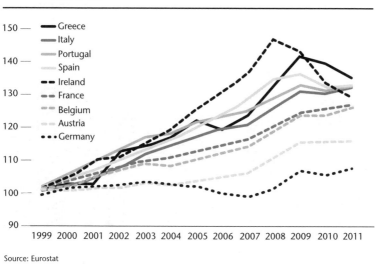

Source: Eurostat

in a number of euro zone members since 1999 (we normalise 1999 costs to 100). We see that, by 2008, German real unit labour costs were almost identical to those in 1999, but have subsequently risen about 7 per cent. By contrast, Irish real unit labour costs rose some 46 per cent by 2008 but, by 2011, were only 29 per cent above their 1999 level.

With floating exchange rates such competitiveness differentials would naturally be addressed, at least partly, by currency depreciation or appreciation. Within a currency union, they must instead be addressed by a combination of internal devaluation and fiscal transfers, each of which we shall consider in more detail below.

One should not, however, expect real unit labour costs between different regions of a currency zone to march in lockstep. At any one point in time there may well be relatively cheap and relatively expensive regions.

In Germany, for example, from 1970 to 2004, some *Länder* had unit

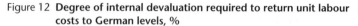

Figure 12 **Degree of internal devaluation required to return unit labour costs to German levels, %**

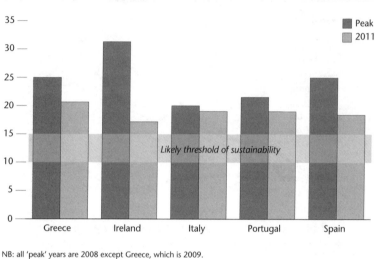

NB: all 'peak' years are 2008 except Greece, which is 2009.
Source: Europe Economics

labour costs falling, relative to the Federal Republic's average change, by around 10 per cent, while others rose 10 per cent.[3] Divergences of +/–5 per cent are typical. Very similar results apply to the USA.[4] This implies that differentials between fastest-rising and slowest-rising regions of more than 10 per cent, and in extreme cases as much as 20 per cent, might well be a natural reflection of adjustments that are quite normal within a single currency area and do not necessarily imply unsustainable divergence.

In Figure 12 we re-present the euro zone data for unit labour costs in a different way.[5]

3   S. Dullien and U. Fritsche, 'How bad is divergence in the Euro Zone? Lessons from the United States of America and Germany', University of Hamburg Department of Economic and Politics Discussion Paper 5/2006, 2006, Table 1: 'Relative nominal unit labour costs in the German Länder'. See http://www.eabcn.org/research/documents/Dullien_Fritsche.pdf.

4   Ibid., Table 6.

5   Note that here we compare unit labour cost trends with those of Germany, thus with the

In constructing this figure, we assume that as at 1999 (i.e. at the commencement of the euro) competitiveness differentials were sustainable, given that they had arisen during a period of separate currencies. During the period of the euro, there has been divergence in unit labour costs relative to this starting point. As can be seen, unit labour costs in Ireland rose more than 30 per cent relative to those in Germany (peaking in 2008) and are still around 17 per cent higher than their 1999 relative level. Italian divergence was much less at peak (20 per cent, again in 2008) but still significant.

This figure suggests that Ireland required a very large internal devaluation as at its 2008 peak, but that much of this has already been achieved. Spain appears to have achieved the second-largest internal devaluation so far, starting as the second-most overvalued (after Ireland), and now has less additional internal devaluation to achieve than Italy, Portugal or Greece. Greece, despite its deep and protracted recession and despite the efforts of its fiscal consolidation so far, has struggled to deliver nearly so great an internal devaluation as Ireland and Spain. Italian and Portuguese labour has become somewhat more expensive over the lifetime of the euro, relative to Germany, and has fallen back but probably has farther to go.

As noted above, though these figures suggest that there may be further need for internal devaluation, they should not be taken as implying that internal devaluation must continue until the differential is zero. The largest within-currency-area relative deviations of around 20 per cent involved relative costs in some regions falling, relative to the average, by around 10 per cent, while those in others rose, relative to the average, by around 10 per cent. Of course, although relative movements of up to 20 per cent might occur even within long-established currency areas, that does not mean that such large movements are sustainable over the long term. Perhaps,

---

slowest-rising region of the euro zone, not with the euro zone average. Note also that by 'German levels' we refer, as above, to the German post-1999 trend rather than to the absolute level of unit costs – so costs would 'reach German levels' if they matched the same percentage change since 1999 as the percentage change in Germany.

therefore, the natural expectation should be that truly sustainable deviations might be closer to the 10 per cent suggested as more typical within historical single-currency countries such as the USA or Germany.[6]

If we leave open the possibility that some deviation beyond 10 per cent might be sustainable and assume that relative deviations of 10–15 per cent could be possible while a situation close to equilibrium was maintained (as indicated by the shaded zone in Figure 12), it appears that there might potentially be a need for limited internal devaluation in Ireland (perhaps as little as 2 per cent) while further adjustment is probably required for Italy, Portugal and Spain (at least 3 to 8 per cent). The necessary adjustment for Greece is at least 6 to 11 per cent (and potentially much larger) – at least one and a half to three times as much as it has already achieved. As such, it is worth examining the question, how best is adjustment achieved?

Internal versus external devaluations
The advantages of exchange rate movements

When countries face fiscal crises that trigger IMF intervention, a classic package is to combine spending cuts with a large currency devaluation, restoring competitiveness and allowing the economy to grow in domestic currency terms. Of course, in international money terms the economy contracts dramatically, but the process allows equilibrium to be achieved with relatively little unemployment, mitigating the social impacts and risk of disorder.

---

6   Additional caveats could be added here. The previous studies on Germany and the USA did not take as their starting point a situation where these single currency zones were new, so any change in competitiveness of regions could have been correcting for earlier changes or in addition to earlier changes depending on the direction of competitiveness changes before the beginning of these studies. Also, just because changes in competitiveness of the order of +/–10 per cent may be sustainable in particular cases, it does not follow that they are sustainable in the particular case of Germany and Greece (or other indebted countries). Furthermore, currencies were not freely floating before the euro zone was formed. It is likely, however, that unsustainable competitive disequilibria would have put unbearable strains on the fixed-rate system that preceded the creation of the euro.

Without a currency devaluation, adjustment to the new equilibrium must be achieved by nominal prices and wages and asset values falling in the country concerned. This is often referred to as an 'internal devaluation' since it – eventually – achieves the same real-terms effects as a currency devaluation, but via internal price changes.

Internal devaluation is usually regarded as a more expensive way to adjust real-terms prices within a country relative to its trading partners for three key reasons. Firstly, it involves changing many prices rather than just one (the exchange rate). Thus, economists say it involves high 'menu costs'. Secondly, prices are often believed to be 'sticky downwards' – that is to say, it is easier to raise prices and wages than to cut them. In an internal devaluation, prices and wages may need to fall in nominal terms. This can be challenging to achieve, and may involve strikes and riots and other expensive consequences which are likely to make the situation worse. Furthermore, the reduction in internal prices may be achievable only via unemployment and company failure, leading to the cost of resources being idle. Thirdly, in respect of domestic currency loans from one citizen or institution of a country to another, an external devaluation leaves loan burdens fairly constant – the real value of loans falls (in international currency terms) but the real value of wages in international currency terms also falls. When there is an internal devaluation, the burden of debts, even from one citizen or institution to another, rises because wages fall, but already accumulated debts remain the same. That means there can be more defaults in an internal devaluation, creating additional costs of bankruptcy.

It is well established that exchange rate adjustments allow the absorbing of shocks with lower variance in consumption (smaller recessions) than internal devaluations.[7] Of course, the question of whether maintaining a fixed exchange rate induces superior policy responses in

---

7   For example, see M. Devereux and C. Engel, 'Fixed vs floating exchange rates: how price setting affects the optimal choice of exchange rate', NBER Working Paper 6867, 1998, http://www.nber.org/papers/w6867.pdf.

other respects (such as inflation control) than floating rates is another matter discussed below.[8]

Balancing short-term gains against the loss of long-term reform

The question is, to what extent might floating exchange rates have helped to absorb the shocks to the countries which are now in difficulties. Applying the model of Devereux and Engel suggests that floating exchange rates could have mitigated losses in GDP, in real domestic terms, of around 5–9 per cent (in some cases by preventing GDP from having risen that far above trend in the first place).[9] It should be observed, however, that for some member states in the euro zone (for example, Ireland) the bulk of these losses have already been taken – so further gains from exiting the euro might be limited. In other cases, where GDP had already risen well above sustainable levels, GDP must fall (the country must become poorer) – the only question is how.

On the other hand, there would be significant long-term consequences and risks for countries exiting the euro. In the first instance, for some euro zone members (especially Greece and Cyprus), their membership of the euro is deeply connected with the country's long-term geopolitical and cultural positioning. In the case of Greece, euro membership is widely regarded as defining whether Greece is to be a Western country like France or Italy, or a Balkans country like Albania and Serbia, or even an eastern Mediterranean country like Turkey, Syria and Egypt. Furthermore, the process of exit itself presents considerable challenges, discussed in other chapters.

Assuming that the mechanics of exit could be managed, and focusing on economic issues, it is possible that exiting the euro and devaluing could

---

8   For example, see J. Aziz, 'Fixed or flexible? Getting the exchange rate right in the 1990s', IMF Economic Issues no. 13, 1998.

9   The author would be happy to explain these calculations to correspondents. The argument from the paper is technical. Given the well-known capacity of floating exchange rates to absorb economic shocks when there are sticky prices, however, this out-turn does seem reasonable.

create a buffer, allowing exiting countries an opportunity to implement structural reforms. But it is also possible that devaluation could be a short-term expedient allowing exiting countries to avoid structural reforms. The consequence of weaker euro members exiting and devaluing could be a build-up of pressure for further decline in exchange rate values and relaxation into accepting a steady decline in wealth relative to their neighbours – with higher inflation, lower competitiveness and lower real growth. A key potential benefit of the euro was that it was supposed to eventually force countries to face up to the need for structural reform and fiscal discipline in ways that domestic politics had struggled to achieve, and to manage inflation better than domestic policy anchors had been able to achieve before. On this account, to exit the euro now would be to surrender at what might be a moment of victory.

An alternative possibility is that some exiting countries could benefit from hanging on inside the euro until the last minute, and then leaving. The analogy here is with the analysis sometimes offered in relation to the UK's experience of the ERM. The common tale with regard to the ERM is either that the UK should never have joined or that it joined at the wrong parity, and so suffered from its membership, with growth occurring on exit. But there is a school of thought according to which UK membership of the ERM served its purpose of crushing the last vestiges of the UK's inflationary presumptions of the 1970s and 1980s, and that exit occurred at precisely the right moment – when growth could occur without inflation.

In an analogous way there might be a school of thought according to which some euro zone members would have gained all the key politico-cultural benefits of euro membership (in terms of inducing an appetite for structural reform, fiscal discipline and low inflation) and thus that a euro exit would not now produce the inflation and retardation of structural reforms often feared.

What has been the past currency experience of euro members when addressing deficit and debt issues?

A common policy package, when delivering significant fiscal adjustments, is to combine fiscal tightening with monetary loosening. Such monetary loosening would be expected to be associated with depreciation in the exchange rate more rapid than trend.[10] It is of interest to consider how, for euro members, fiscal adjustments in the past have been associated with exchange rate movements. In Figure 13 we compare changes in fiscal balances versus changes in exchange rates, for a selection of countries, in the period before the euro.

For Belgium we see that for most of the period there was fiscal tightening (in 1981 Belgium had a deficit of more than 15 per cent of GDP, which dropped gradually and continually to a little over 2 per cent by 1997) and fiscal tightening was associated with exchange rate weakness. For Greece the early 1980s and the 1990s had the expected pattern, but the late 1980s to early 1990s saw much less exchange rate movement than the average of the period as a whole.

From the late 1980s and through the 1990s, Spain had the expected pattern (when the deficit is falling the exchange rate weakens more than usual, and vice versa) but, through most of the 1980s, there was no such correlation.

For Ireland, the early 1980s, early 1990s and the late 1990s show the expected pattern – other periods do not.

Portugal shows the expected pattern for almost all of the period.

For the period for which we have data, Italy does not show the expected pattern.

Thus in Belgium, Ireland, Greece and Portugal it has been normal for exchange rate movements to be significantly correlated with changes in the deficit. It is worth noting, however, that exchange rate depreciation versus the Deutschmark was much less for Belgium and Ireland than for other countries in our sample (indeed, for an extended period in the

---

10 A fiscal tightening could, itself, contribute to an exchange rate depreciation if lower capital flows from abroad were necessary to finance government borrowing.

Figure 13 **Correlation between changes in fiscal balance and changes in exchange rate**

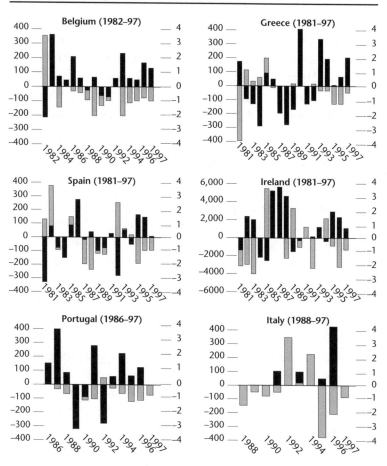

■ Change in exchange rate vs DM relative to underlying change, 1981–2003
■ Change in fiscal balance (% of GDP)

NB: the left-hand axis is percentage movement in the currencies' exchange rates versus the Deutschmark, from the year indicated to the following year, relative to the average movement in exchange rates for the period 1981–98. The right-hand axis is the change in the fiscal balance as a percentage of GDP. When the columns are on opposite sides of the horizontal axis, this means that a reduction in the deficit was associated with a relatively weak period for the currency, or vice versa. When columns are on the same side of the horizontal axis, this is not so.
Source: Europe Economics analysis on Federal Reserve and IMF data

early 1980s the punt actually appreciated versus the mark). The average annual depreciation for the Belgian franc was a little over 1 per cent per annum and for the punt a little under 1 per cent per annum. For the escudo average annual depreciation was about 7.5 per cent and for the drachma nearly 9 per cent. Thus, although there has been correlation for Belgium and Ireland, it has been much less material than for Greece and Portugal. For Spain and Italy it is much less clear that their economies would naturally require depreciation to accommodate fiscal tightening.

A fiscal transfer union, but not a debt union

Since the euro was first proposed, it was recognised that for it to function there would need to be significant fiscal transfers as there are within other currency unions. Such transfers limit the degree to which competitiveness differentials must be dealt with by internal devaluation or labour mobility. They thus increase the political sustainability of a currency union, by allowing regions of the currency union to avoid or limit periods of high regional unemployment which are often associated with internal devaluation or large population movements as people abandon regions with low competitiveness.

Most commentary on the euro zone crisis recognises the need for such fiscal transfers or 'fiscal union'. Discussion of the meaning of a fiscal union is confused, however. Most commentary has fixated upon the idea that a fiscal union implies sharing past debts. Not only is the sharing of debts not the only kind of fiscal union, but it would not help with the euro's structural flaws and would actually make things much worse.

In a fiscal union, such as the UK or the USA, taxes are set centrally and then transfers are made to help out regions. For example, every year folk in London pay taxes so that money can be sent to Liverpool, raising the wealth of Liverpudlians above that which they would deliver for themselves. Such regional transfers are absolutely necessary if the euro zone is to survive and flourish. German taxpayers will have to pay taxes, every year, so that money can be sent to Spain and Italy to make the Spanish and Italians wealthier than they would deliver for themselves.

Such regional transfers within the euro zone would not involve any profound departure of principle from current and past policy. At present, every year, there are about €60 billion of 'structural and cohesion funds' paid from wealthier parts of the EU to less wealthy parts. To make the euro zone work that amount would have to rise, but probably not by more than around €20–€40 billion. An additional €20 billion would, for example, raise the output of Italy and Portugal by around 1 per cent.

What does not happen in other currency unions – and what would not be necessary or appropriate or even helpful for the euro zone, either – is for wealthy parts of countries to guarantees debts raised in less wealthy parts. The Greater London Authority does not guarantee the debts of Liverpool City Council, for example. And no one would suggest that doing so is necessary for the 'sterling area' to function. Indeed, quite the opposite – if London did guarantee the debts of Liverpool, that could be quite destabilising to the sterling area. For in that case Liverpool City Council would have incentives to overspend and over-borrow and under-tax – imposing a burden on Londoners that they might not feel happy bearing. This is the problem often described as 'moral hazard'. The guaranteeing of debts is likely to lead to governments (whether local governments in the UK or national governments in the euro zone) spending more and borrowing more than would otherwise be the case.

A similar scenario exists when people visiting a restaurant decide to split the bill. When we each pay for our own dinner at a restaurant, we decide what we want to eat, bearing in mind the cost to us of our choices. Similarly, when the government of an individual member state of the euro zone or an individual local authority within a country (such as Liverpool City Council) pays interest on its own debts, it decides how much to spend and borrow (and how much to bear the political costs involved in reforming labour markets and other parts of the economy in ways that promote growth), bearing in mind the cost of its choices.

But when diners split the food bill in a restaurant, or the governments of the euro zone split the interest cost bill in a debt union, those incentives change because we do not face the full cost of our decisions. In a restaurant, this can be referred to as the 'lobster problem' – everyone ends up ordering the lobster.

How significant is this lobster problem? This question was addressed in a well-known academic study in the *Economic Journal* in 2004.[11] The authors conducted experiments with diners (strangers to one another), some of whom paid individually while others split the bill. Those that split the bill spent about 36 per cent more than those that paid individually, while if someone else paid the bill well over twice as much was spent.

Conversely, in order to mitigate the risk of such an overspend, Londoners might demand oversight of Liverpool City Council's spending and taxation decisions, impinging on the democratic process of Liverpudlian elections. This can be termed the 'vassal problem'. A recipient region becomes the vassal of the debt-guaranteeing region.

Since neither side would be happy with that arrangement, there would be a natural tendency for both to want to break up the sterling area to get away from the arrangement.

What is true for Liverpool and London is all the more true for Germany and Italy. It is not a necessary part of any fiscal union between Germany and Italy that Germany guarantees the debts of Italians. If they were to do so, that would destabilise the euro and create incentives for both Germany and Italy to leave.

This is an even greater problem when the debts in question are not currently arising debts, but debts that were in place before the euro even existed. It is simply absurd to say that it is somehow integral to the functioning of the euro that Germany must accept responsibility for trillions of euros of debts incurred before it even existed. And it also would not help, because the reason Italy has a problem with its debts

---

11   Gneezy, Haruvy and Yafe, 'The inefficiency of splitting the bill', 2004.

is that its growth rate is low. The main driver of low Italian growth is not high debt, but low competitiveness within the euro. That fundamental problem would simply reassert itself, given enough time, even if Germany were to pay all Italy's debts off and even if (*mirabile dictu*) Italy were not to overspend if someone else were picking up the tab.

For the euro to function there needs to be fiscal union, which does not mean debt pooling. It means year-on-year transfers from high-growth regions of the euro to low-growth regions, offsetting the competitiveness and balance of payments issues that would otherwise be addressed via currency depreciation.

Conclusion

This chapter has argued that balance of payments issues within the euro zone should primarily be seen as the symptom of other issues:

- Some degree of natural shifts in relative competitiveness within the euro zone of the sort that has occurred in the past in other currency unions, such as the dollar and the Deutschmark.
- Mistaken assumptions about the relative future growth and stability of different euro zone regions.
- Unsustainable debt accumulation policies of governments.

We have seen that internal devaluation is likely to be an expensive mechanism, in GDP loss terms, for achieving sustainable competitiveness, debt and balance of payments positions, compared with the alternative of currency depreciation, but that, for some member states of the euro, their geopolitical status is bound up with euro membership. For other member states, euro membership was intended to discipline policymaking. Hence euro departure would, for some countries, involve considerable medium-term policy risks, even if the considerable challenges of the transition itself could be met.

Furthermore, some euro members have already made considerable progress down the internal devaluation path and have already borne a significant element of the associated GDP costs. This means that departure at this point may be of less benefit than would have perhaps been the case in, say, 2009. Not all euro members are in the same position with respect to past experience in achieving internal devaluations and correcting government deficits without accelerated currency depreciation. During the 1980s and 1990s, Italy and Spain, in particular, did not tend to experience accelerated currency depreciation in periods of fiscal consolidation.

Over the longer term, it is likely that competitiveness and balance of payments issues within the euro area will, if the area is to survive, need to be mitigated by larger and more specific fiscal transfers than the present system of structural and cohesion funds. Such a system of fiscal transfers should, however, if it is to be useful, be focused upon regular and sustained future flows of funds, not the guaranteeing of debts accumulated before the euro even existed – a process that is in no way necessary for the successful functioning of currency unions and which would risk destroying the euro area altogether.

6 SAVING MONETARY UNION? A MARKET SOLUTION FOR THE ORDERLY SUSPENSION OF GREECE

Pedro Schwartz with Francisco Cabrillo and Juan E. Castañeda

The Greek misadventure has given birth to mistaken remedies that have neither healed Greece nor stopped contagion. The original design of the euro, as the only legal tender currency in the euro zone, has turned out to be socially and politically costly. It implies transforming nominal convergence of deeply diverse economies into real convergence. Simply bailing out an errant member, while imposing ill-planned expenditure cuts and inordinate tax increases, is turning out to be counterproductive. More generally, the attempt to keep ailing members within the euro against all the odds is endangering European Economic and Monetary Union (EMU) and even the EU itself. The interested parties are at loggerheads as to what to do to save the single currency. The debtors want mutualisation of sovereign debts; the creditors resist any mitigation of the rules governing the European Central Bank (ECB). Despair is setting in. Even if one thinks that monetary union was a good idea to start with, a collapse of the euro now would result in painful monetary chaos.

The mismanagement of the Greek crisis could turn out to be a blessing. Expelling Greece from the euro system is legally difficult if not impossible. For the Greeks to leave the euro zone voluntarily is also complicated: they would have to exit the EU and then return as an aspiring member of EMU on the same terms as recent new entrants. There is another way. The euro could be made a competing currency alongside national currencies. The solution may sound outlandish to many but it is similar to John Major's 'hard ecu' proposal. In 1990, the then Chancellor of the Exchequer, John Major, proposed a common European currency instead of a single currency. It would have been electronic money to be used by business and tourists. Its value would initially have been equal to a basket of EU currencies but it could not subsequently have been devalued relative to any member currency. This would have made it as hard as the hardest member currency. Major's idea was rejected, but we now see that it could have saved us from the present troubles.

Why not consider a temporary suspension of EMU membership and allow Greece to reissue drachmas while keeping the euro in circulation? Greece could be rescued from its plight by running drachmas and euros in parallel, fully convertible at floating rates. This would allow it to heal its economy while not forsaking the euro project. Such a move would have to be carefully designed but is feasible. Bank deposits in euros would have to be guaranteed to avoid a bank run – the main cost of the scheme though a dwindling one. True, foreign debts expressed in euros would become an extra burden on banks and on mortgagees, but those debts could be alleviated along the well-tried lines of the Club de Paris for sovereign debt and the London Club for private debts. The main advantage for Greece would be that pricing wages, taxes, social benefits and domestic assets in drachmas would help make the Greek economy competitive in foreign markets and achieve the necessary price adjustments. By not forsaking the euro totally, balance of payments deficits would continue to be financed for the time being as at present by Target 2. Greek banks could have recourse in moments of need to both the ECB and the Greek central bank. The drachma need not disappear if the Greek central bank applied a conservative monetary policy – indeed, the central bank would have an incentive not to misbehave if it wished to maintain its seigniorage income. A full return to the euro could be contemplated at a later stage, if Greece wanted this.

Why is the euro failing?

A stable currency is an important factor in the prosperity of a country. In the long run the denomination of the money matters little since, given time, individuals and firms will adjust prices and wages to changes in currency values. In the short term, however, life can be made very difficult by changes in the value of money. The euro had been designed as a stable currency, independent of the real and credit circumstances of different member countries. In its first ten years both price stability and low transactions costs were beneficial. The fact that there was some degree of free-riding by countries unwilling to play by the rules was not thought to be of great importance.

The present crisis has shown otherwise. In the boom years euro interest rates had been managed by the ECB following the example of the Federal Reserve. They were too low even for Germany, where their effect was to exaggerate the export capacity of its economy. They were certainly low for the rest of the euro zone. Since asset prices tend to vary inversely with interest rates, cheap money led to steep rises in asset values and there was an incentive to invest imprudently. Low rates also induced people to run excessive debts, as ever-rising asset prices made all investments appear riskless for lenders and for borrowers. With interest rates of the whole area converging on the German rate, governments, firms and households in deficit countries felt able to borrow abroad without limit. All this led to long periods during which debtor countries had little incentive to reduce costs and improve productivity.

Thus it is that the pro-cyclical policies of the central bank in a monetary zone can cause what is known as a 'bubble': the CPI price level may be stable for a while when money supply is expanding, but asset values keep rising for as long as the real yield of the 'overpriced' assets does not disappoint investors' expectations. Once those expectations turn, the financial crisis sets in. The natural consequence should have been sovereign defaults and private bankruptcies. Failures need not become systemic as long as the money supply is maintained by the central bank.[1] Furthermore, the rule of the Maastricht Treaty was that

---

1   Ever since Friedman and Schwartz (1963) we have known that it is crucial that in a crisis central banks act as lenders of last resort and abide by the Bagehot rule (1999 [1873]) of lending money to solvent banks at punitive rates. Congdon (2011) applies the Friedman

there should be no bailouts. When this rule was not obeyed, contagion of the whole euro zone was unavoidable.

The euro zone was not an optimal currency area

For five or six years the euro seemed to be functioning well despite the fact that the euro zone was not an optimal currency area, as Mundell (1961) defined the term. This was not thought to matter, since Mundell taught that monetary zones with a single currency could exist even if they differed in economic structure, under two conditions: firstly, easily transferable or movable factor services; and, secondly, flexible prices and wages. If factors of production could move easily from one occupation to another and from one location to another, then a fall in demand for a product in one place or industry could be compensated directly by factors moving to another place or activity. There would be no need to use the exchange rate to return to full employment. Equally, immobile factors could stay in their original employment if wages and prices were so flexible that the local market always cleared. In any case, he added, direct adaptation through wages and prices was not so different from adaptation to economic shocks through the exchange rate. The only difference, he thought, was one of perception or money illusion.

The experience of EMU, however, has shown that it is not money illusion which makes some countries prefer devaluations to cost-cutting. If European governments often hanker after the possibility of devaluing it is because differences in language, nationality, unionisation, welfare entitlements, taxation, property rights and so on hinder the easy movement and the realistic pricing of factor services.

Suboptimal currency areas are not static. Areas can come closer to optimality through structural changes leading to greater factor mobility, real exchange rate convergence and openness to foreign markets.[2] Unfor-

---

and Schwartz warning against falls in the quantity of bank money to the present situation.

2   Vaubel (1978: 64–71) proposed that we take the divergence of real exchange rates in the various regions as an index of how low the optimality of the currency area is.

tunately, the creation of the euro zone by itself has not visibly fostered factor mobility and structural convergence. Despite all efforts to create a single market in the EU, barriers remain and have even grown through the very regulations intended to bring them down.

When exchange rates are fixed (as they are in a monetary union) and capital movements are free, a government has only one remaining policy instrument left if any at all – fiscal policy.[3] In the last resort, activist governments will want to stimulate their economy despite the evidence that increased public expenditure financed with sovereign debt is ineffective in the long run. To guard against the temptation for governments to spend for electoral purposes the founder members of the euro signed the 'Stability and Growth Pact' in 1997. Unfortunately it was watered down in 2005. Seeing its ineffectiveness, a new 'euro-plus pact' was drawn up in 2011. Reactions to the present crisis make one doubt that such agreements can stop governments from trying to escape the discipline of the single currency.

The euro as politics

Ultimately, the euro is a political project for state-building and not a way of opening the EU to the world. The enormous efforts to save Greece and others show how far euro zone leaders are ready to go it together. They think all would be well with a more executive, functioning, integrated, protected and powerful European Union. To the disappointment of all concerned, the Greek quagmire is slowly sucking in the single currency ... and its passengers.

---

3   This is what has come to be known as the Mundell trilemma, which states that only two of fixed exchange rates, open capital markets and monetary sovereignty can be attained. A government, when exchange rates have been fixed, can exercise monetary sovereignty only if it places strict controls on capital movements. Since, in EMU, internal capital controls are forbidden, the only remaining policy instrument is fiscal. However, the inertia of tax and expenditure policies blunts this instrument.

Two lessons from the past

The real and the pseudo gold standard

To have adopted the euro is often likened to functioning under a classical gold standard. In both cases a country gives up two important macroeconomic tools, the management of the rate of exchange and the possibility of running a chronic budget deficit. In gold standard years the Bank of England used interest rates simply to speed up the adjustment of the economy when there was a loss or accrual of gold. When domestic banking crises occurred, the Bank of England acted as a lender of last resort. There was no need for a political authority to govern this automatic system. Under the euro the ECB enjoys a margin of safety even the Bank of England did not have in the second half of the nineteenth century. The ECB is not bound by its reserves of metal but by a much more flexible rule that consumer price inflation has to be kept below but close to 2 per cent per year. The (nominal) bank rate can be used to decrease or increase the money supply. Euro zone member states still have fiscal policy as a macroeconomic instrument, but recourse to budget deficits was in theory limited under the Stability and Growth Pact. At one point it was intended that the ECB should be as independent as the Bank of England: by design the original euro system was not supposed to need a central political authority.

When fragile peace was restored to Europe in the 1920s the larger countries returned to gold, but the standard was made to work differently to how it did before World War I: the only currency directly linked to gold was the US dollar; the others were simply kept at a fixed exchange rate to the dollar. As the Great Depression struck, one by one countries gave up even this 'exchange gold standard'. The fundamental reason for giving up gold was that the pre-World War I parity of the national currency to gold implied deflations that proved unfeasible, given the habits and institutions of twentieth-century societies. As Keynes said in August 1931 when the devaluation of sterling with respect to gold was being discussed: 'our choice lies between devaluation, a tariff

... and a drastic reduction of all salaries and incomes in terms of money'.[4] Keynes's phrase accurately portrays the plight of Greece and other euro zone nations today, barred from devaluing, from controlling capital movements and also finding internal devaluation well-nigh impossible. Only the three Baltic republics have shown the mettle to make the euro work in a crisis. Making the euro a solid and stable currency for the other European nations is proving just as difficult as the use of gold in the 1930s.

What is it that makes the classical gold standard impractical in our unionised welfare societies? The classic gold standard has an element of imposition or central regulation that prevents it from being a completely free market currency. The rate of exchange of the pound, the dollar and the franc was fixed to gold effectively by decree. The result was that note circulation was governed by gold reserves. To compete in world markets nations had to have to resort to deep cost-cutting. The same can be said of the euro.

Milton Friedman in 1961 proposed another form of gold standard, one from which we can draw inspiration in the euro zone: a 'real' gold standard contrasted with the 'pseudo' gold standard of classical times, as he called it. Gold certificates would circulate as currency if people freely preferred to use them in their contracts. The certificates would be issued by institutions holding gold deposits, institutions that would be separate from the central bank issuing the local currency.

> Side by side with such a standard, there could, of course, exist strictly national currencies. For example, in the United States from 1862 to 1879, greenbacks were such a national currency which circulated side by side with gold. Since there was a free market in gold, the price of gold in terms of greenbacks varied from day to day. (Friedman, 1987 [1961]: 456)

The only conditions needed for such a flexible gold standard to function would be that the rate of exchange between paper and gold

---

4   Keynes (1982), p. 605.

would be flexible, not fixed; exchange and capital movements must be totally free; and legal tender should be abolished so that contracts and tax payments could be made in gold or paper or any other money that people freely chose.

This analysis can be applied to the parallel currency system that we propose for Greece. The euro, well anchored by the issue rule of a truly independent central bank, could circulate side by side with national money. Crucially, the ECB would issue euros based on a credible monetary standard (a 'hard euro') and would not act like a conventional national central bank, but merely be the issuer of a parallel hard currency. In this scenario, the 'new ECB' would not implement monetary policy decisions to achieve any macro goal or to 'drive' the growth of the economy. Public administrations, firms and private individuals would freely choose in what currency to denominate their taxes, obligations and contracts. The competition with the euro would discipline the local central bank. This system could be used not only in Greece but in any member country that had to go back to its national currency.

The shambles of the currency board in Argentina

The disorderly exit of Argentina from a decade-long currency board arrangement is a strong warning of what could happen to Greece if it were suddenly forced to exit the euro by a wave of speculation.

A history of repeated inflation had led the Argentinian government to set up a currency board in 1991 permanently linking the peso with the US dollar at a one-to-one exchange rate. It lasted for a little over ten years. During those ten years the conditions for a well-functioning currency board were flouted with catastrophic consequences. Those conditions are that the local currency must be fully convertible; the central bank may not finance spending by domestic governments; and the central bank must have reserves at hand that cover 100–115 per cent of the domestic monetary base. Convertibility was held for as long as possible but disregard for the second condition fatally undermined the system: the public deficits of the state and provinces led to monetisation of the debt. Dollar reserves melted as confidence dwindled and the board was nearing collapse.

In 2001, a recently elected President De la Rúa, having inherited a fiscal deficit of $7,350 million, tried to save convertibility by further deflating an economy already stagnant for two years. He called back Domingo Cavallo, the founder of the currency board, who tried to stem growing capital flight. After $18 billion had left the country during the first eleven months of 2001, Cavallo tried to rebuild confidence by having the government pass a 'zero deficit law' and an 'intangibility of deposits law'. Still fearing a run on the currency, he also called on the IMF for what we would today call 'big bazooka' help, but this simply increased the alarm of investors.

Cavallo then imposed what many specialists think will be necessary if Greece or another EMU member is forced to leave the euro overnight: he ring-fenced the money market, with what Argentinians immediately called the 'cattle pen' or '*corralito*'. To stop the bank run individuals were not allowed to withdraw more than $200 in cash per week or transfer more than that amount abroad without central bank permission. Even so, in the first quarter of 2002, bank current accounts shrank by 25 per cent and GDP fell by a further 45 per cent. De la Rúa and Cavallo resigned. The new interim president, Duhalde, first devalued the peso by 50 per cent. He then decreed that deposit holders could withdraw their frozen dollar assets in pesos at the rate of 1.40 peso per $1 and that dollar loans owed to banks could be repaid in devalued pesos at the favourable rate of 1 peso per dollar. To save banks from collapse the government gave them bonds equal to the value of their loss due to devaluation. Finally a new president of the country defaulted on $132 billion of foreign debt. Growth ensued but inflation soon returned.

What happened in Argentina is clearly a warning to European authorities facing a possible Greek default. If nothing is done, a moment will come when commercial banks in a besieged country will suffer a sudden liquidity crunch. An overnight *corralito* would have to be imposed. This would very quickly reflect on the real economy, especially if the Target interbank, inter-country transfer system were to shut down overnight. The economy would then become moneyless and would grind to a halt.

The chaotic euro zone non-exit strategy
Direct and indirect costs of keeping Greece afloat

Keeping Greece within the fold of the euro by piecemeal measures instead of radical and immediate remedies has entailed direct and indirect costs which are increasing by the month. These costs are centred not only on Greece but also on those other countries in the euro zone suffering from the repercussions of the Greek bankruptcy.

The direct costs include the loans to bail out Greece (€240 billion committed of which €150 billion has been paid out), Ireland (€67.5 billion), Portugal (€78 billion) and now Spanish banks (a €100 billion facility out of which €35 billion is to be paid out immediately). A total of €485 billion has been promised and €330.5 billion spent. There are also costs implicit in the debt guarantees proffered by the EU at a level of more than €600 billion.[5] In addition, the ECB has greatly expanded and will go on expanding its balance sheet by purchasing bonds of doubtful quality. It has also promised to buy sovereign debt on the secondary market, with the pretext that the ensuing interest rate reduction would increase the efficiency of the monetary policy transmission mechanism.

Many of the bailout loans come with frills attached. In the case of Greece, for example, when in November of last year it was granted the third instalment of its €240 billion facility amounting to €34.4 billion, a number of further concessions were made: the period of past loans was extended by two years, their rate of interest reduced to 0.5 per cent above the three-month Euribor rate, and a further €9.6 billion was promised for a debt buy-back operation.[6] All these concessions have

---

5   Public debt data from Eurostat (as available up to November 2012).
6   Greek debt is trading at 35 cents on the euro, a sizeable discount. It is probable that

been calculated to amount to a further cost of at least €32.6 billion (Stravis, 2012).

The indirect costs include the insurance premiums or spreads paid by the less credible countries: this has meant an increase in sovereign bond interest payments for Greece, Portugal, Ireland, Spain and Italy to the sum of €28 billion. Also, there are costs that are difficult to measure, such as the loss of confidence in EU institutions, mainly the ECB, owing to the amount of bad paper in the ECB portfolio.

Prevarication to avoid a write-down

As at December 2012, Greek debt amounts to €301 billion. A write-down of 53.5 per cent was imposed on the holdings of private banks in the first bailout agreement in October 2011. With the proposed debt buy-back, holders wishing to sell will suffer another haircut since the current discount of Greek bonds on the market is 35 cents on the euro. In the agreement of November 2012, granting the third tranche of the €240 billion facility, official institutions have been exempted from taking a cut on their Greek debt holdings, which means that taxpayer-backed institutions, though holding 70.5 per cent of Greek debt, have been exempt from haircuts. The ECB holds €36 billion of Greek debt and marking it to market would draw a question mark over the whole of its portfolio and perhaps force a recapitalisation – a politically embarrassing move, especially for Germany.

Parallel currencies and transition problems

The parallel currencies system we propose will be different from Major's hard ecu proposal or a classical currency board. The drachma and the euro would be on a clean float and neither would need to be legal tender.

---

holders of bonds issued under English law will keep them to maturity (Open Europe blog, 28 November 2012). Also, the German finance minister, Wolfgang Schäuble, is on record as saying that there would be no new loans for the buy-back (Stravis, 2012).

This means that Greece or any other European country deciding to follow this route will not have to exit the euro zone. How this parallel currencies system will function is more fully described below, but the problems that could arise in the transition must first be analysed.

Avoiding a run on deposits after suspension

The whole scheme that we propose could founder if a bank run developed. Money, as is well known, performs three functions: it is a standard by which to compare the relative value of goods and services; it reduces the cost of exchanging goods and services; and it can be a store of value for future use. So the stable value of money is a condition for a well-functioning economy.

Today, around 85 per cent of a country's money supply is bank deposits in financial institutions. The 15 per cent cash reserve backing banknotes is thus 'fractional'. When depositors lose confidence in the bank that keeps their money, the bank will find itself without enough cash to satisfy their calls. It may not be able to realise its other assets and panic may ensue. Such a flight to cash will leave the economy without ready means for transactions and cause a steep fall in production. If Greek holders of euro accounts fear their deposits will suddenly be redenominated in devalued drachmas they will try to convert them into euro notes immediately or send them abroad. Panic will ensue. This is the reason why experts say that any plan to expel a member from EMU has to take deposit holders by surprise and be preceded by capital controls (see the chapter by Neil Record). Gros (2012) has suggested a simple way to suspend the free movement of capital without resorting to border controls or the prohibition of money transfers. It would be enough to suspend the automatic functioning of the European interbank clearing system Target 2, so that Greek resident banks would be unable to charge money transfers to other European banks. All these measures take away one of the essential freedoms of the European Common Market and should be avoided.

One way of preventing a run would be fully to guarantee deposits in euros. The cost of a 100 per cent deposit guarantee in Greece would have been less than the transfers squandered by the non-exit strategy (the narrowly defined €130 billion or the total commitment of €240 billion seen above). In January 2012 the total amount of bank deposits in Greece was €225.25 billion. It will have fallen further by now. The total guarantee of those deposits would not have cost that much since only the difference between the value of the deposits before and after devaluation would have to be met. In fact, the €240 billion committed so far to the Greek non-exit strategy would have covered the greater part of the cost of guaranteeing Greek bank deposits in euros.

Keeping commercial banks solvent

Of course this would create problems for the solvency of Greek banks. However, the only help that is needed is to keep the euro denomination of deposits. In our proposal, loans to the private sector and those pension fund assets invested in bank deposits would be redenominated in drachmas. Since public debt would, in any case, have to be restructured by way of a substantial 'haircut' for creditors, it is not important for banks whether or not it is redenominated in drachmas. As such, for the sovereign bonds owned by banks a menu of two options could be offered: an issue of new bonds in euros with, let us say, a 50 per cent reduction in their nominal value; or a redenomination of public debt in drachmas maintaining their nominal value. The effects would be the same for the banks' balance sheets.

With regard to the non-financial private sector, their bank deposits would not be re-denominated in drachmas, but mortgages and other loans from banks to the private sector would have to be re-denominated to maintain the solvency of the majority of households and firms as wages would be paid in drachmas. Since the general public holds about €225 billion of bank deposits which would remain in euro, but banks' assets would be redenominated, the banks would need substantial financial assistance from foreign governments and international financial institutions.

In sum the total cost of the suspension of Greece to set up a system of parallel currencies would be the cost of keeping their *deposits* denominated in euros and of being content to recover the value of their euro *credits* in drachmas. The exact amount of the aid commercial banks needed would depend on how much the drachma devalued.

The gainers from this process would be Greek citizens, who (in aggregate) maintain the euro value of deposits but have their borrowing transformed into drachmas. Given this, we would also suggest the introduction of a new windfall tax on the withdrawal of funds from euro-denominated deposits. This should not be a general tax on financial transactions, but a temporary tax for the specific purpose of helping to keep Greek banks solvent to be paid by people withdrawing money from their deposits in euros. This will serve several purposes. Firstly, it would reduce windfall profits obtained by Greek residents with bank deposits in euros; secondly, it would create incentives to delay withdrawals from deposits in euros and thus reduce the possibility of bank runs; finally it would help finance subsidies that banks would receive from the government for having to redenominate their credits in drachmas.

How much devaluation?

How large a devaluation of its new currency would Greece suffer before finding its appropriate level? Several calculations have been made. Nouriel Roubini estimates that the euro is overvalued in Greece by at least 30 per cent.[7] Michael Hart, using unit labour cost levels, suggests that, to eliminate its current account deficit, Greece should devalue by 50 per cent and even more to enter a sustainable growth path.[8] Nomura

---

7   *Financial Times*, 22 November 2011.
8   RGE Share, 26 September 2011.

Bank calculated in 2011 that the value of European currencies in a euro break-up scenario needed to fall in the region of 60 per cent for Greece, around 50 per cent for Portugal and 25–35 per cent for several countries, including Ireland, Italy, Belgium and Spain.[9] In any case it is very difficult to determine the equilibrium exchange rate for a currency *ex ante*. Also, in an exit scenario, there may be some overshooting. But we can assume that 50 per cent is a reasonable extent of the necessary devaluation of the new Greek drachma. Therefore, capital losses on assets newly denominated in drachmas can be estimated at 50 per cent. Also, Greek residents will find it very difficult to pay back private euro debts after devaluation, so that some means of settling defaults would have to be found.

The Shylock syndrome

The exit of a nation from a currency board arrangement or from a monetary union is usually accompanied or even preceded by a large default, be it direct or by devaluation (see Reinhart and Rogoff, 2009, 2011). Up to the 1970s the settlement of foreign defaults was left to the markets. In the last third of the twentieth century defaults of sovereign debt were settled in Brady Bonds, which at present are touted for Greek-like situations.

In 1988, Treasury Secretary Nicholas Brady proposed his eponymous plan whereby banks that had lent too much to Latin American states 'voluntarily' accepted to receive a smaller amount in bonds on condition that debtor countries would open and free up their over-regulated markets. The plan worked with the help of loans from international organisations and a US Treasury guarantee for those new bonds, so

9   Nomura, in what it calls a 'redenomination scenario', takes into consideration both real exchange rate current misalignments and future inflation risk, measured by four parameters: sovereign default risk, inflation pass-through, capital flow vulnerability and past inflation track record. See Niki Kitsantonis, 22 January 2012, http://topics.nytimes.com/top/news/international/countriesandterritories/greece/index.html, accessed 23 January 2012.

that disappointed creditors were at least able to trade their paper on the international market.[10]

There are, however, private ways of dealing with default that are more conducive to the ultimate recovery of defaulting countries, which ensure that costs do not fall on the shoulders of creditor countries' taxpayers. Some intermediaries are for-profit companies, such as the World Debt Corporation. Others are informal organisations that have emerged in the second half of the last century where creditors meet failing debtors: the Paris Club for sovereign creditors and the London Club for private creditors. From the mid-1950s the Paris Club has assisted in the sovereign debt restructuring of more than eighty countries. More than four hundred agreements have been reached; and total debt covered in the framework of Paris Club agreements amounts to more than $550 billion. The London Club has also reached a large number of debt reconciliations. This includes, among others, the private debts of Serbia and of Soviet Russia.

People have often argued against private settlement of defaulting sovereign debt as giving debtors too much bargaining power. Experience shows, however, that creditors can strengthen their negotiating positions by (a) keeping their loans current for as long as possible; (b) closing the door to further credit; (c) restructuring their loans with debt-for-equity swaps, debt buy-backs, debt exchanges, debt-for-bond swaps, and settlement of debts; and (d) buying their claims at a discount in local currency and using them to purchase equity in the debtor countries. Debtors too, if they hold foreign currency reserves, can repurchase their own debt at depressed market value and thus indirectly obtain a reduction in their indebtedness.

Lenders have a strong incentive to find the amount of debt reduction that will maximise the recovery of a failing nation. A creditor may very often benefit from forgiving some debt, so that payments of interest and principal do not strangle the debtor. Shylock had much reason to

---

10 See Ian Vásquez's (1996) summary of the scheme applied to Mexico in 1989.

hate Antonio and Christians in general. His contract with Antonio was valid. But by claiming his pound of flesh he lost all – the ducats, a fair daughter and the desired revenge. Sometimes it is better to pardon than to receive.

The proposed monetary regime
Parallel currencies with no legal tender

With a parallel currency regime, residents, banks and governments would still be able to use the euro. Commercial banks especially would keep their connection with the ECB as well as with the new drachma central bank: i.e. both central banks would act as lenders of last resort along Bagehot lines. Neither currency needs be legal tender. European politicians and officials will want to reject this solution of floating parallel currencies for its apparent untidiness, however, for fear of competitive devaluations and because 'it has never been tried'.

Free competition always looks untidy to the planner. We are highly sceptical of the supposed benefits of competitive devaluations without capital controls as there would simply be either open or repressed inflation. It is notable that in the years after the Civil War, when greenbacks and gold certificates circulated in parallel, as explained by Friedman and Schwartz (1963) and Friedman (1987 [1961]), American dealers engaging in large foreign transactions maintained both gold balances and greenback balances in New York banks. The 'greenback dollar' and the 'gold dollar' constituted 'a dual monetary standard'. Their relative value was determined in a free market. That is why they could coexist side by side without either driving the other one out.[11]

If people are free to choose the money they prefer, monetary

---

11 If residents are forced to use currencies that are exchangeable only at a fixed rate, bad money will displace good by the effect of Gresham's law. 'Gresham's law that cheap money drives out dear money applies only when there is a fixed rate of exchange between the two. It therefore explains how greenbacks drove out subsidiary silver. [... S]ilver could still have stayed in circulation, as gold could and did, by being accepted at its market value rather than its nominal value' (Friedman and Schwartz, 1963: ch. 2, n. 16).

competition will make convergence towards better currencies easier. As Vaubel (1978: 68–9) said in his path-breaking study, choice on the *demand side* of financial services makes for stable money. Over time, people tend to grow out of the illusion that inflation leads to growth. Also, choice in currency will bring the monetary area nearer to optimum size. And there will be a demand for a conservative monetary policy in relation to the new drachma because of the availability of the euro as an alternative – especially for savers. Supply side oligopolists may try to exploit money illusion.

It is clear that drachmas would be used in parallel with euros so long as they float freely and neither is legal tender. The euro will not push conservatively managed drachmas out of circulation or reduce them to the role of small change.[12]

A temporary reserve for the new drachma

As the new drachma floated freely against the euro and residents freely chose which of the currencies to use, the drachma would in the end find its level. In the first flush of distrust, however, there could be a great deal of volatility and possibly even rejection of the new currency. The example of Estonia could be followed. It decided to have a currency board arrangement with the euro, guaranteeing the solidity of its kroon fixed exchange rate by using its forests as a reserve asset. Along these lines, the Greek government could pledge state properties as a temporary guarantee for its new drachma. Alternatively the Bank of Greece could earmark its tourist income as a guarantee in the same way that the Spanish Habsburgs made over the income of their '*alcabalas*' or sales taxes to their German and Genoese bankers.[13]

---

12 Sargent and Velde (2002: ch. 14, especially fig. 14.1).

13 The Bank of Greece recorded its high-powered money as €21,687 million in September 2012. If we assume a devaluation of 50 to 60 per cent when starting to issue new drachmas, the circulation of the new currency will be in the range of ND8,575 million to ND13,012 million. The tourist income of the Bank of Greece was €10,505 million in 2011. This amount translated into new drachmas at the assumed devaluation would more than

One can reasonably assume that, once the initial uncertainty was over, a conservative monetary policy on the part of the Greek authorities would stabilise the purchasing power of the new drachma.

Two clubs in competition

Two banking clubs in competition[14] would provide the central banks at their head with the right incentives to offer the best services to their members. In this new scenario, the commercial banks of the suspended country would have the choice to be members of – and obey the rules of – either or both clubs. In essence, they will move their deposits according to the quality of the services provided by each currency, measured in terms of the ability to preserve purchasing power in the medium to long term. In the absence of obstacles posed by legal tender and capital controls, and in a world dominated by instant communication, competition in the money issue market is a real possibility.[15] Additionally, with increased competition, there would be no incentive for explicit or implicit collusion between the two issuers of money, as there is today in the central bankers' oligopoly.

The Greek national bank would perform the following functions.

- Issue its own currency.
- Act as one of the two suppliers of liquidity to the monetary system.
- Provide different clearing facilities to the bank members of its club.
- Purvey regular and extraordinary credit as needed.

Self-interest would drive the new Greek monetary authority to

cover the new drachma's MO.

14　See Goodhart (1988), where he defines the role of central banks as heads of clubs of commercial banks with powers to inspect and duty to lend in the last resort.

15　The benefits of monetary competition are receiving increasing attention among economists. Starting with Hayek (1976), there is quite an extensive literature on this question (among others, White, 1984, and Selgin, 1988). See King (1999) as well, when he was the deputy governor of the Bank of England.

control money growth and inflation. The commercial banks of the suspended country would presumably be members of both clubs: they still should have access to Target 2, the euro-wide clearing facility, as well as to the national clearing facilities in drachmas. Greek banks would also have the choice of receiving regular credit from the ECB in euros, as they would have deposits and investments in both currencies. The ECB would accept as collateral sovereign debt denominated in either euros or drachmas valued at market prices with appropriate haircuts. This would make both bonds in euros and in drachmas tradable in financial markets. The initial exchange rate of the national currency would be subject to high volatility just after launch but then would settle down, when the market started to perceive that sound fiscal and monetary rules were being followed.

A central bank's target will be to maximise its seigniorage in the long term. Since the seigniorage associated with money issue ultimately depends on the demand for the currency, the national monetary authority would soon feel that an inflationary fiscal and monetary policy mix was hurting it as individuals and commercial companies moved to the more stable currency, the euro.

A new fiscal policy in the suspended country

Fiscal discipline will be reinforced by the need to have the drachma compete with the euro. In order to defend the drachma, there must be a truly binding fiscal rule that must include:

- A specific fiscal target.
- A time horizon to evaluate the achievement of the target.
- Exposure of the government in office in case of a deviation from the target.
- Timely and transparent accountability measures to make sanctions effective.

- Greece should leave the euro temporarily.
- A new drachma would be issued allowing the circulation of the euro at a freely floating exchange rate.
- Exchange and capital controls would not be necessary to avoid a run on Greek banks as deposits in euros would be guaranteed.
- Liabilities of the Greek state and all Greek residents would be redenominated in drachmas.
- Arrangements such as the Club of Paris and the Club of London could be reached on euro-denominated private and public debt.
- Parallel circulation of euros and drachmas would encourage the Bank of Greece not to over-issue and the Greek Treasury not to overspend, under pain of shrinking seigniorage.
- Parallel circulation might slowly lead the Greeks back into full membership of the euro zone if they so wanted, by the free choice of Greek residents and businesses.

All this could include regular hearings in parliament, open letters between the prime minister and the governor of the central bank in the case of discrepancy, and a required adjustment plan with specific measures and a timetable to achieve the pre-announced goal.

A summary of the whole process is provided in the box above.

Conclusion and wider implications for remaining members of the euro zone

A parallel currency approach to the Greek situation would not involve amendment of the treaties, since temporary suspension is not equivalent to a country voluntarily or forcibly leaving the euro. The approach would be market-driven and create currency competition and a new dynamic towards decentralisation. It could also be achieved at much lower cost than the costs of deferring exit that are currently being incurred.

The temporary suspension of a member of the euro zone, however, would increase the speculation already taking place against other vulnerable members. Hence, such a move would pose a dilemma for EU and national authorities. They could either allow parallel currency circulation in other failing countries or they could impose an immediate and drastic programme of fiscal consolidation of the kind applied by the three Baltic countries. As noted, the Greek experience shows how tardy and expensive the second solution can be. The other fringe members of the euro zone are also finding the fiscal consolidation way politically difficult – and this includes Spain and Italy. The lesson may be that forcibly keeping a country in the euro will end in failure.

It is a fact that attitudes towards the euro differ sharply in the core and the fringe members of the euro zone. The group headed by Germany would like to have the zone abide by the original EU treaties, including the no-bailout clause, and see the ECB committed again to long-term price stability. The ECB is performing de facto as a conventional central bank, however, and thus is also committed to rescuing states in crisis and supporting its own currency. Also, the fringe members are asking for full bailouts when needed and an accommodating monetary policy. Such a divergence is endangering European unity and the consequent indecision will cost the taxpayer a great deal of money.

The best way out of this quandary is to allow parallel currency exit for all members of the euro zone that wish to use it. Those members who want a solid euro should demand monetary management along classical lines from the ECB, with the ECB becoming, once again, fully independent. The stronger countries should also allow the weaker members to issue their old currencies anew in free competition with a well-managed euro. The availability of a credible and well-defined exit strategy for failing countries would help alleviate pressures on the whole euro zone. This solution requires that EU politicians put the welfare of Europeans ahead of the objective of making the EU a single-currency world power.

References

Bagehot, W. (1999 [1873]), *Lombard Street. A Description of the Money Market*, London: John Wiley & Sons, Inc.

Congdon, T. (2001), *Money in a Free Society: Keynes, Friedman, and the New Crisis in Capitalism*, San Francisco: Encounter Books.

Einaudi, L. (2001), *Money and Politics. European Monetary Unification and the International Gold Standard (1865–1873)*, Oxford: Oxford University Press.

European Central Bank (2008), 'Ten Years of TARGET and the launch of TARGET 2', *ECB Monthly Bulletin*, November.

Friedman, M. (1987 [1953]), 'The case for flexible exchange rates', in *Essays in Positive Economics*, Chicago, IL: University of Chicago Press. Reprinted in Kurt R. Leube, *The Essence of Friedman*, Stanford, CA: Hoover Institution.

Friedman, M. (1987 [1961]), 'Real and pseudo gold standards', *Journal of Law and Economics*, 4, October, pp. 66–79. Reprinted in Kurt R. Leube, *The Essence of Friedman*, Stanford, CA: Hoover Institution.

Friedman, M. and A. Schwartz (1963), *A Monetary History of the United States, 1857–1960*, NBER and Princeton University Press.

Goodhart, C. A. E. (1988), *The Evolution of Central Banks*, MIT Press.

Gros, D. (2012), *How to Avoid a Greek Exit and Still Establish Price Signals*, CEPS Commentary, Summer.

Hart, M. (2011), 'Valuing the new Greek drachma', RGE Share.

Hayek, F. A. (2008 [1976]), *Denationalisation of Money*, London: Institute of Economic Affairs.

Keynes, J. M. (1982), 'The 1931 financial crisis', *Activities 1929–1931*, ed. D. Moggridge, in *The Collected Works of John Maynard Keynes*, vol. XX, Macmillan and Cambridge University Press.

King, M. (1999), 'Challenges for monetary policy: new and old', Presented at the Jackson Hole Conference 'New challenges for monetary policy', Federal Reserve Bank of Kansas City, August.

Mundell, R. (1961), 'A theory of optimum currency areas', *American Economic Review*, 51(4): 657–65.

Reinhart, C. M. and K. S. Rogoff (2009), *This Time Is Different. Eight Centuries of Financial Folly*, Princeton, NJ: Princeton University Press.

Reinhart, C. M. and K. S. Rogoff (2011), 'From financial crash to debt crisis', *American Economic Review*, vol. 101(5): 1676–1706.

Roubini, N. (2011), 'Greece should default and abandon the Euro', *Financial Times*, 19 September and 22 November.

Sargent, T. J. and F. R. Velde (2002), *The Big Problem of Small Change*, Princeton, NJ: Princeton University Press.

Selgin, G. A. (1988), *The Theory of Free Banking: Money Supply under Competitive Note Issue*, Totowa, NJ: Rowman and Littlefield (also at the Online Library of Liberty).

Stravis, M. (2012), 'Greek debt deal explained', 'Brussels Beat', *Wall Street Journal*, 27 November.

Vásquez, I. (1996), 'The Brady Plan and market based solutions to debt crises', *Cato Journal*, XVI(2): 233–43.

Vaubel, R. (1978), *Strategies for Currency Unification: The Economics of Currency Competition and the Case for a European Parallel Currency*, Tübingen: J. C. B. Mohr.

White, L. H. (1984), *Free Banking in Britain: Theory, Experience and Debate, 1800–1845*, Cambridge: Cambridge University Press.

White, L. H. (1999), *The Theory of Monetary Institutions*, Oxford: Blackwell.

Wikipedia, 'Greek sovereign crisis', downloaded throughout November 2012.

7 MANAGING THE TRANSITION – A PRACTICAL EXIT STRATEGY

Neil Record

Introduction

This chapter looks at the practical issues of a euro exit, and the steps that member states, and the EU institutions, should take to manage this effectively.

A euro exit will be seen as catastrophic among much of the EU establishment, and for many will herald the end of the 'European Project', which has been moving forward since the Treaty of Rome in 1957. It is partly, even mainly, because this project has been an article of faith for so many of the EU elite that the economic and financial failures of the euro have been glossed over, covered up or denied since the failures began to emerge early in the euro's life, say around 2003. This inability to contemplate that the euro may have fatal flaws will make the practical suggestions made in this chapter particularly hard to consider for many Europeans, and even harder to implement. The chapter does not therefore indicate what the author expects to happen but details the political actions that would minimise the financial cost and maximise the economic benefit of euro exit.

Summary of the exit route

The recommended route requires the formation of a secret German task force. Absolute secrecy and deniability are essential because, if the markets get wind of any plans for the dismantling of the euro zone in its current form, then events will accelerate and spiral out of control, rendering the task force's plans irrelevant.

This task force should develop a plan that envisages the first exit being the only exit – namely the complete abandonment of the euro when it becomes inevitable that one member is to leave. This approach is suggested only with reluctance. The complete abandonment of the euro would be a momentous step for euro zone members, and would mark the end of the integrationist project for the EU.

The alternative of piecemeal departures would lead to a situation where the view that the euro is 'unbreakable' or 'permanent' is untenable. This would give markets the evidence and the ammunition to continue to turn their fire on euro structural weaknesses elsewhere. This is a recipe for a continuing crisis, resolved only when the last target that the market can find is demolished. In practice, this would be the enforced slow-motion dismemberment of the euro.

The plan
Implications of exit

It is not likely to be possible for the EU or any of its institutions to conduct a planning exercise of euro-self-destruction. As such, Germany, as the effective guarantor of the 'Eurosystem',[1] is the only country with sufficient power and authority within the euro zone to be able to plan a future for all euro zone members. Therefore, Germany alone should constitute a secret task force to plan for euro exit.

It may be that this task force's plans (and indeed the existence of the task force) never see the light of day. It may be that the plans need to be brought to the Council of Ministers only in 2015. It may be that they are needed immediately.

Currently there remains a strong strand of belief (particularly in

---

1   The 'Eurosystem' is the colloquial name for the combined grouping of the European Central Bank (ECB) and the seventeen national central banks (NCBs) of the euro zone. The 'European System of Central Banks' (ESCB) is the 'Eurosystem' plus the ten non-euro-zone-member NCBs.

euro zone countries) that exit is impossible.[2] As we have already seen in 2010–12, markets are constantly probing and re-evaluating the probabilities and scale of alternative outcomes, and managing their investment and derivative positions accordingly. To date, most of the market pricing of euro stress has been concentrated in the sovereign debt markets. But this represents just one of two risks within the euro – the risk of sovereign default. The other risk – the risk of redenomination (or 'intra-euro currency risk') – has so far found little direct expression in the markets.

With a euro exit, this belief would be shattered and, once that happened, almost all of the advantages that a single currency had over an exchange rate mechanism would evaporate. It is likely, if there are any exits from the euro zone, that markets will begin to discriminate in favour of 'strong' (predominantly northern) debtors and against weak (predominantly southern) debtors on the basis of perceived exit risk. This could lead to a rapid emasculation of southern countries' banking systems as southern depositors moved their deposits north for little or no cost or loss of interest.

An effective plan also needs to ensure that redenomination disputes for 'stateless assets' do not become a catalyst to damage fatally both the relevant financial systems and the ability of commercial companies to operate in a stable framework. This issue will be discussed below.

Complete euro abandonment

The only way to prevent contagion-mediated slow-motion euro disintegration, together with ruinous litigation over stateless assets, is to announce the complete abandonment of the euro on the first exit.

The euro zone has created a series of unique problems for the management of an exit. At the forefront of these is the euro zone banking system, and bank balance sheets that are currently denominated in

---

2   '… As I see it, the Bundesbank's Target2 claims do not constitute a risk in themselves because I believe the idea that monetary union may fall apart is quite absurd …'. Dr Jens Weidmann, president of the Deutsche Bundesbank, Open Letter, 13 March 2012.

euros. The exact scale of the damage that an exit would wreak on individual banking balance sheets depends on a number of factors. First and foremost is the choice of redenomination rules for assets and liabilities. Here, the following course of action is proposed to deal with these problems. When a country leaves the euro it makes the following core decisions in relation to redenomination:

- All bank accounts at banks/branches which are located in the country are redenominated in the new national currency. The nationality or residence of the customer is not taken into account. The residence, therefore, of the *debtor* (not the creditor) is the determining factor in determining redenomination (but see the mortgage exception below).
- All national contracts, labour agreements, pensions, savings, share prices, bond prices and house prices are redenominated into the new national currency.
- All mortgages secured on property within a departing country are redenominated into the new currency. The residence of the borrower is deemed to be irrelevant – denomination goes with the location of the mortgaged property.

To the extent that this treatment is under the exiting country's control, uncertainty can be contained or eliminated. But a bank in an exiting country that owns a foreign asset (for example, an Italian bank owning French government bonds) will not be able to have them redenominated into the exiting country's new currency. They will remain in euros, or indeed themselves be redenominated into the currency of the borrower (French francs in this case) if further fragmentation takes place. So, as a general rule, it seems likely that much or most of the liability side of banks' balance sheets will be redenominated at exit, but that only the domestic element of the asset side will be redenominated.

If this rule is followed, many large, stronger-country banks (based mainly in Germany, the Netherlands, France and Austria) will become insolvent without government assistance. This is because at least some of their assets will be located in weaker euro zone countries, whereas all of their domestic liabilities will be redenominated into their national (strong) currency. It should be made abundantly clear in the exit announcement that the governments and national central banks of their respective countries are standing fully behind each of these banks and providing unlimited liquidity at the moment of exit and its immediate aftermath. In the immediate aftermath of the announcement, liquidity provision is evidently of the utmost importance to prevent bank runs and collapses. In the longer term, respective governments will have to decide which parties bear the bank losses arising from euro zone break-up, and the extent to which these are socialised. The lessons of the 2008 banking crisis probably mean that governments will bail out depositors, but not necessarily other bank creditors and bond-holders. Of course, different governments may make different decisions regarding this issue.

The ECB – a major systemic risk

The ECB is a very unusual central bank, in that it does not have a single government sponsor. For all major developed countries with their own currencies, the national central banks are, in effect, an arm of government, and are treated by the markets as if they were the government of the relevant country.

Under normal circumstances, the ECB would not pose a particular threat to the European financial system. Its main remit is to control European inflation by exercising monetary policy – in effect setting euro interest rates.[3]

Since the start 'proper' of the euro crisis in 2010, however, the ECB has been providing core funding to a large number of euro zone banks that

---

3   'The primary objective of the ECB's monetary policy is to maintain price stability. The ECB aims at inflation rates of below, but close to, 2% over the medium term.' ECB, http://www.ecb.int/mopo/html/index.en.html.

cannot fund themselves except at ruinously high interest rates, or indeed at all. In effect, southern banks have been shunned by investors; these banks have turned to the ECB for funding, with the ECB in turn funding itself with deposits from northern banks flush with cash and with no secure assets to invest in.

The liabilities on the Eurosystem balance sheet at 15 June 2012 (which includes at the time of writing the ECB proper to an unknown extent, and netting off intra-system transactions and assets/liabilities, such as Target 2 – see below) stood at €3.03 trillion.[4] This is 32 per cent of euro zone GDP – an alarmingly large number for a thinly capitalised multilateral institution, with vulnerable sovereign assets, which could be subject to redenomination in the event of a euro break-up.

Target 2

The ECB is also responsible for Target 2. This was designed as an integrated euro zone payments and clearing system, in many respects equivalent to Fedwire in the USA.[5] Rather to the surprise of Target 2's designers, since the start of the financial crisis in 2007, Target 2 has also acted as an 'automatic' lending system to weaker countries' banking systems, not just a clearing system.

The Dutch Central Bank explains it well:[6]

> Target2 is the payment system enabling direct transfers between commercial banks in the Euro zone ... If the banks in a particular euro country are net receivers of cross-border payments via Target2, this results in that country's NCB [national central bank] having a claim on the ECB, which acts as the central counterparty within the Eurosystem. The NCB in a euro country with a net

---

4   'Monetary policy statistics', Table 1.1: 'Consolidated financial statement of the Eurosystem', *ECB Monthly Bulletin*, 15 June 2012.

5   For more information on Fedwire, see http://www.federalreserve.gov/paymentsystems/fedfunds_about.htm.

6   De Nederlandsche Bank, 'Target2 balances: indicator of the intensity of the European debt crisis', 12 April 2012.

Figure 14 **Germany's net Target 2 position**
Euros, billion

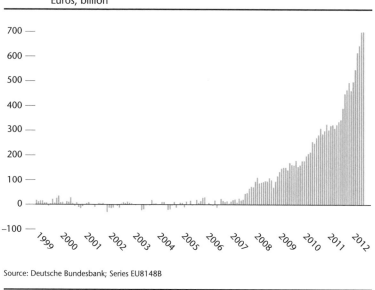

Source: Deutsche Bundesbank; Series EU8148B

payment outflow will have a liability to the ECB. The accounting entries representing the amounts that NCBs owe to or are owed by the ECB are referred to as 'Target2 balances'.

The issue of Target 2 balances would not matter much, were it not for the burgeoning balances that are now evident. Figure 14 shows the Bundesbank's credit balance in the Target 2 system as at 31 May 2012. The latest balance is €698 billion, which is 27 per cent of German GDP, and rising rapidly. The Dutch credit is a similar percentage of GDP, but, for Luxembourg, the Target 2 balance was about 250 per cent of GDP at end-2011.

These flows represent a combination of capital flight and accumulated northern trade surpluses.

In Figure 15, I have illustrated this cumulative trade surplus for Germany versus the rest of the euro zone. This shows that the orders of magnitude of the April 2012 German Target 2 balance and the

Figure 15 **German cumulative trade surplus with euro zone**
Euros, billion

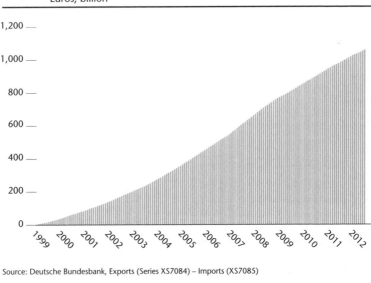

Source: Deutsche Bundesbank, Exports (Series XS7084) – Imports (XS7085)

cumulative trade surplus from January 1999 to February 2012 are similar.[7]

If a country wishes to import more than it exports, it must borrow money to do so (or sell existing assets). In trade across currency blocs, it must also buy foreign currency and sell its own to willing private sector participants. If this is not possible a country simply cannot run an external (trade) deficit.

Inside the euro zone, it is different. A euro zone country whose private sector is importing more than it exports does need to borrow money, but it does not need to sell or lend its own currency in favour of

---

7   The data in Figure 15 are just the trade surplus (cumulative exports by Germany to the rest of the euro zone less cumulative imports from the euro zone), not the full balance of payments, which is not available for this trading pair. For Germany, the trade balance and the balance of payments including services, net interest and dividends are not that dissimilar.

a foreign currency. Until 2007, it appears from the Target 2 balance data that deficit (southern) countries were successful in borrowing from the private sector (to the tune of some €600 billion) so that the respective central banks were able to clear all their cross-border euro transactions and stay in balance. Since 2007, southern states have found it difficult or impossible to attract voluntary private sector lenders willing and able to lend money to them in sufficient quantity to cover their trade deficits. Indeed, there has been an unwinding of previous loans so that in June 2012 the privately funded gap between the cumulative German trade surplus and Target 2 was €320 billion and falling. Instead of private sector loans, the southern banks are, in effect, borrowing from the ECB financed by northern banking system loans to the ECB via the national central banks.

There is no reason why the private sector should not continue to extract itself from all lending to southern countries, leaving only the national central banking systems, supported by ever-rising Target 2 balances, to fund them. One way or another, this puts the taxpayers of the respective euro zone countries at very substantial risk should there be an exit. Should there be a southern exit and redenomination, then either the northern national central banks or the northern private sector banks that are lending to their national central banks, or the ECB, will have losses inflicted upon them. Of course, the euro zone countries provide the capital to the ECB. Furthermore, if northern private sector banks became insolvent it is likely, in practice, that sovereign governments would become liable for some of their indebtedness.

Effect of euro abandonment on stateless 'euros'

If the euro continues in existence, then there will be billions of euros of contracts, of debt and of other instruments operating under non-euro-zone law, which will continue, in the legal sense, to be obligations of the contracting parties.

On complete euro abandonment, however, such frustrated euro

contracts, with no natural domicile, could, with the agreement of the parties, be valued and terminated using an ecu (European Currency Unit) calculation. Since the euro would be no longer deliverable, it seems possible that (at the behest of the EU) both the USA and the UK (and other relevant, supportive jurisdictions) could enact legislation that allowed their courts to value outstanding contracts using a newly defined ecu[8] basket representing the value of the defunct euro, and, if delivery was the only option, to deliver the basket.

New ecu basket for termination or run-off valuation

The euro's constituents have expanded since its foundation in 1999. Only ten current euro zone member states' currencies were represented in the ecu, which was abandoned at the end of 1998.

The task force needs to design a fair currency basket instrument, which would command the support of the banking, business and legal community, and which would provide termination and run-off value to the myriad of derivatives and other 'stateless' euro contracts, debt and assets outstanding at the time of writing. The obvious weights for the new ecu should be the adjusted ECB capital key which determines the effective shareholding (and loss-bearing) weights of the ECB.

Under full break-up, on the first day of trading following exit, each of the new national currencies will be priced by the market relative to the US dollar. The international value of the ecu would vary according to the independent market pricing of each new national currency relative to the dollar. But, with this new ecu mechanism, there could be a transparent and fully independent market-based resolution and run-off pricing mechanism for all stateless euros.

Table 2 shows an illustration of how the ecu basket might be

---

8   At the moment of creation of the euro, the old ecu ceased to exist, converting to the euro at 1:1. At that moment, its value was a weighted basket of fixed amounts of twelve EU currencies, nine of which joined the euro on 1 January 1999. The others were the UK, Denmark and Greece (which joined in 2001).

calculated using a US dollar/euro exchange rate of 1.25 US dollars per euro both before and after a full break-up. In column E in the table, arbitrary assumptions have been made about possible appreciation and depreciation of the new national currencies for illustrative purposes only.

Exit and transition timetable

Once one member has concluded that they (or other members of the euro zone) wish for them to exit, either through 'force' or through choice, and this decision has become irreversible, then, following the recommendations above, Germany would need to activate the task force plan. Any variations from this plan will be limited or constrained by necessity.

The moment an exit becomes inevitable, Germany would call a Council of Ministers meeting (ideally on a Friday evening – but that may not be possible) which would take place that night between EU Heads of Government. It need not be a fully physical meeting.

Germany will reveal to member states' leaders the existence of the task force and the outline of its exit plan. Germany will have to ask the Council of Ministers' assent for the plan. Current treaty provisions would not permit the plan in theory, but the political reality is that, if the Council of Ministers agrees, they can decide in due course to amend existing treaties and associated domestic legislation to give their decisions legal force at a later date.

Germany's backstop will be to suggest that, if there is no agreement from the Council of Ministers, they will unilaterally withdraw from the euro, and unilaterally announce the activation of a German-only task force exit plan. This will be discussed later.

Assuming that Germany achieves the agreement it needs, at that moment the exit announcement should be made (perhaps early on a Saturday morning).

The initial announcement need only be quite short:

Table 2 **Possible construction of the new ecu**

Country (currency)	A National currency entry/exit rate per euro	B ECB adjusted capital key	C = A x B Currency amount per ecu	D = A / 1.25 US$ exchange rate at official entry/exit rates. US$/ euro rate at exit = (e.g.) 1.25	E Illustrative % change in market value of national currency	F = D / (1 + E) Example post-exit market exchange rates vs US$	G = C / F US$ value of ecu's constituents	H = G / Total G New ecu market weights %
Belgium (franc)	40.34	3.47%	1.40	32.27	0%	32.27	0.04	3.47%
Germany (mark)	1.96	27.06%	0.53	1.56	35%	1.16	0.46	36.54%
Estonia (kroon)	15.65	0.26%	0.04	12.52	–10%	13.91	0.003	0.23%
Ireland (punt)	0.79	1.59%	0.01	0.63	–30%	0.90	0.01	1.11%
Greece (drachma)	340.75	2.81%	9.57	272.60	–50%	545.20	0.02	1.40%
Spain (peseta)	166.39	11.87%	19.75	133.11	–30%	190.16	0.10	8.31%
France (franc)	6.56	20.32%	1.33	5.25	0%	5.25	0.25	20.33%
Italy (lira)	1,936.27	17.86%	345.81	1549.02	–20%	1936.27	0.18	14.29%
Cyprus (pound)	0.59	0.20%	0.001	0.47	–40%	0.78	0.002	0.12%
Luxembourg (franc)	40.34	0.25%	0.10	32.27	0%	32.27	0.003	0.25%
Malta (lira)	0.43	0.09%	0.0004	0.34	–25%	0.46	0.0008	0.07%

Netherlands (guilder)	2.20	5.70%	0.13	1.76	10%	1.60	0.08	6.27%
Austria (schilling)	13.76	2.78%	0.38	11.01	5%	10.48	0.04	2.91%
Portugal (escudo)	200.48	2.50%	5.02	160.39	–35%	246.75	0.02	1.63%
Slovenia (tolar)	239.64	0.47%	1.13	191.71	–15%	225.54	0.005	0.40%
Slovakia (koruna)	30.13	0.99%	0.30	24.10	–20%	30.13	0.01	0.79%
Finland (markka)	5.95	1.79%	0.11	4.76	5%	4.53	0.02	1.88%
Total		100%				US$ value of ecu = 1.25		100%

- From the moment of the announcement, the euro no longer exists.
- Each state will revert, with immediate effect, to its previous national currency, converted from euros at the entry rate into the euro.[9]
- All euro banknotes are no longer euros: they will become fractional denominations of their respective national currencies, the currency being determined by the prefix on the banknotes. This will also apply to coins, which are more easily identifiable. Only nationally issued euro notes and coins are legal tender in each respective country. Foreign-issued euro notes and coins will have to be exchanged at a bank for domestically issued notes and coins at market exchange rates.[10]
- All bank current and savings accounts held in each euro zone country are redenominated into national currencies at the official exchange rate with immediate effect. The official exchange rate is the rate at which each national currency entered the euro. The domicile of the *creditor* of any bank account is irrelevant to its denomination; the only relevant test is the domicile of the branch of the bank (the *debtor*) which operates the account. 'Stateless' bank accounts held outside the euro zone, but denominated in euros, will be converted to an ecu-weighted basket of currencies.
- All other commercial and financial contracts, including labour contracts, pensions and insurance and savings contracts, loan and debt contracts, will be redenominated according to the legal domicile of the contract – i.e. *lex monetae* shall apply. In the absence of clear determination, the default position will be determined

---

9   This is just for convenience – any state could choose different currency names and exchange rates, but for the market to be able to react quickly and with confidence, this seems an appropriate default.

10 It is evidently not ideal to have a small identifying prefix on a note's serial number as the sole determinant of its value. If it is felt that the confusion would be too great, however, it could alternatively be decided that all euro notes and coins, irrespective of origin, could become new ecus – a basket of currencies, exchangeable at market rates for national currency notes when they become available, or for paying into national currency bank accounts at any time (again, at market foreign exchange rates). There is little difference in aggregate between these two alternatives, but a substantial difference at the micro-level.

by the country of domicile of the issuer of the obligation (i.e. the debtor).

- Residential mortgages will be redenominated into the currency of the location of the mortgaged property (breaching the 'domicile of the debtor principle' just for this asset class).

- Each national central bank will provide unlimited liquidity to its own banks – all customer money in euro zone banks is therefore secure.

- New notes and coins will be printed and issued as soon as possible, but euro notes and coins will be legal tender for at least one year.[11]

- There will be a two-day bank holiday in the EU on Monday and Tuesday. Shops and commercial premises are welcome to open, but they must be aware of the new value of notes, coins and bank accounts.

- From Wednesday, banks will reopen, and there will be no exchange controls, and no limitation on cash or deposit withdrawal. Notes, coins and bank accounts can move freely across the exchanges, but all parties must be aware that exchanging different-prefix notes is a foreign exchange transaction and that moving a bank account to another former euro zone country is also a foreign exchange transaction.

- From the moment of the announcement, the ECB ceases to function as a central bank and all its functions are transferred to the respective national central banks. The European Financial Stability Facility and the European Stability Mechanism are abolished, and any commitments and assets they have are repatriated to their respective national governments.

- [If possible …] The respective governments of all non-euro-zone EU member states, and the USA, Japan, Canada, Australia, Hong Kong, Singapore, etc., have agreed to facilitate as far as possible the same treatment for legacy euro contracts as specified above. Genuinely

---

11   The period should be as short as possible commensurate with secure printing and distribution of new national currency notes and coins. One year is arbitrary.

'stateless' contracts will be closed and settled, if possible, using a basket with currency weights of the newly specified ecu, and at market exchange rates and interest rates on the first Friday[12] after exit, and thereafter, if necessary, on subsequent official settlement days.

The task force would have a detailed, hour-by-hour plan of the practical steps to make all of this a reality. There are several parameters above on which the task force would have to make announcements. The ideas above are not set in tablets of stone – they are just examples of the clarity that would be required.

There will undoubtedly be major teething problems with such a large financial convulsion in such a short space of time. There will be unintended consequences that create unforeseen problems, but once the first step of the transition is completed, the next several steps are in much more familiar territory.

A German-only back-up plan

Germany needs to ask the proposed task force to prepare a secondary plan that deals with its possible failure to secure euro zone agreement to the principal plan from the task force.

This plan must be credible enough that euro zone members' leaders believe that Germany would follow it through if there is no agreement; it must be evidently less palatable to the non-German euro zone members; and it must be deemed to be acceptable to the German public (although they would have the opportunity to review it only after the fact).

Germany should propose that it unilaterally breaks away from the euro, re-establishes its own national currency, severs its links with the ECB (accepting liabilities and assets pro rata to its 27.1 per cent adjusted capital key), and takes no further part in the resolution of the euro crisis

---

12 Friday (i.e. after three days of post-exit trading) is arbitrary; the gap might have to be longer.

(i.e. adopts a position like the UK). This is a less complex scenario (at least initially) for the task force planners, since it would not require the closure of the ECB and the total abandonment of the euro. Many of the issues of redenomination uncertainty would still arise, but on a smaller scale, simply because only Germany would be involved.

It is already clear from the earlier analysis that German banks would be badly hit by this route, but on balance it is likely that they would not be in a worse situation than with total euro abandonment. The German government would offer the same unlimited liquidity to German banks as in the main plan and would undoubtedly have to shore up the capital position of the largest German banks with new equity (or quasi-equity) capital injections.

It seems unlikely that the euro zone would be able to survive in anything like its present form if Germany were to go it alone in a euro zone departure, and it runs the risk of engendering internecine warfare between former euro zone members. This could herald a new and very dangerous period for Europe and the world, and is therefore to be avoided at all costs. It is unlikely, however, that the other sixteen euro zone members would choose this course.

After the exit

In examining the immediate aftermath of the exit, I make the optimistic assumption that the EU emerges intact, and that the former euro zone members come through without major social and political disorder. Let us start by looking at the end of the first week.

What does success look like in the post-announcement phase?

A successful first week would involve the following:

- A widespread belief among the general population, the markets and the political classes that all the shock and pain have been taken in one hit, and that the future looks viable and stable, with no further major 'bad news' anticipated.

- A belief that the EU can mend itself and survive as a free trade and economic cooperation area – there would be no euro zone nation-to-nation vendettas, and no EU departures.
- Active political and legal support from the USA, China and the UK and the other major non-euro-zone nations: but with no new bailout money.
- An absence of any of the risks listed in the previous section materialising on any scale.
- Major markets (equity, bond and currency markets) are stable with two-way trading prices by Friday of the first week.

Future stability and growth

There is a great temptation among the economics profession to try to nanny the macroeconomic progress of countries. The profession makes policy recommendations that fit the contemporary theoretical framework, even though the profession's track record is at least as bad as many politicians', and possibly worse. The celebrated 1981 open letter to *The Times* from 364 economists[13] to the UK government exhorting it to stimulate demand by fiscal expansion, in contrast to the budget policy of fiscal contraction and tight money, was ignored by the government, which was vindicated by the UK's very strong economic performance in the subsequent ten (and indeed 25) years.

In the aftermath of an exit of one or more euro member states, it

---

13   In April 1981, following the Budget, 364 leading academic economists (certainly a large proportion of the mainstream UK academic economic profession at the time and including Mervyn King, the current governor of the Bank of England) signed a letter strongly criticising the 1981 Budget proposals, which were for monetary restraint and fiscal tightening in a period of recession. Only a handful of (monetary) economists could be found who supported the Budget. UK real per capita growth from 1981 to 1991 (the ten subsequent years) was 2.5 per cent p.a. – a full percentage point p.a. higher than the previous ten years. Source: National Accounts, ONS.

will be the politicians of each country that will choose their respective economic policy. The complexities and tensions of that dynamic decision-making process are way beyond the scope of this chapter. One thing is certain, however. Whether a departing state chooses austerity and fiscal prudence, or inflation and monetary and fiscal laxity, the market will bring moderating forces to bear, ensuring that only what is possible is undertaken, and rapidly feeding back reality to both electorate and politicians alike. Each country's politicians will have to account for their performance only to their own electorate – not to another layer of government in Brussels. This will reunite the democratic process with economic authority and responsibility for policy decisions.

Whatever the arrangements that pertain post-exit, the northern trade-surplus countries (Germany, Netherlands and Finland) will almost certainly find that they lose competitiveness as their currencies appreciate versus the southern states.

This loss of competitiveness will naturally depress aggregate demand, and tend to reduce trade surpluses. Germany in particular has an export mix which is reasonably price-inelastic (dominated by high-quality engineering), so the loss of competitiveness may show a reverse 'J' curve – an initially higher trade surplus as the terms of trade improve, followed by a loss of export volume as the longer-term elasticities take hold. Germany will face the challenge of having to stimulate domestic demand to replace its falling net export demand – and this against a backdrop of a very indebted public sector under almost any of the conceivable scenarios. This has been Japan's problem since 1990 – and it is not easily soluble, though the problem would certainly be mitigated by substantial microeconomic reform and a reduction in taxation along with government spending.

Trade and the EU

It is vital that the single market (or at least a broadly tariff-free market) remains intact in the EU as a whole. Although the single market has not succeeded in spreading to all business sectors (housing; pensions; insurance and financial services generally are some examples), in many areas the single market is working well, and already copes with ten countries within the single market, but outside the euro zone. There is no reason why this cannot continue with all 27 countries having individual currencies.

Nevertheless, the fundamental blow that euro zone break-up will inflict on the EU project should not be underestimated. At the core of the EU there will be deep despondency at the failure of the most important single flagship policy. There is a danger in this environment that the EU could begin a retreat across many fronts, and that the eurosceptics, with their tails in the air, will vigorously pursue a more nationalistic agenda egged on by national politics which will have been shaped by the painful recent experience. This is a recipe for renewed protectionism, for domestic preference, and for all the 'Spanish practices' that prevented fully effective trade in many periods of history.

If we are to avoid a full-blown depression, then it is vital that, in the wake of this enormous political and economic convulsion, the energising force of international trade, and its positive effect on the welfare and wealth of nations, is allowed to flourish. This will be the challenge for a new generation of post-euro politicians.

Conclusion

The euro zone is exhibiting severe stress. The stress is most visible in the form of public sector deficits and debts. In one member state's case (Greece), the debts were so large by March 2012 that they were (partially) defaulted on.

Current euro zone policy is to enforce 'austerity' on the supposedly recidivist southern states, with 'austerity' interpreted as imposing strict fiscal conditions on European bailout money. Demanding fiscal retrenchment at a time of recession, however, is widely seen (particularly in the south) as perverse, exacerbating already weak economies.

Northern private sector investors are no longer prepared to recycle their money to the south, and have also largely withdrawn their existing portfolio investments and loans in the euro zone's south. This means that the public and private sectors in the south now have only one source of funding – the ECB and associated European funding mechanisms.

This emphasis on public sector deficits is misplaced, however. The deficits are a symptom of an underlying problem and not the cause. The underlying problem is that the southern states are running large, invisible, current account (i.e. trade) deficits, and that the normal feedback loop of a falling currency and the repricing of imports and exports is being prevented from operating. So the absorption of aggregate demand that current account deficits imply, together with a shell-shocked domestic private sector in the south that is likely to be net saving and not net borrowing, means that the only source of additional net aggregate demand to square the sector identities that apply in all economies[14] is the public sector. If the public sector attempts to reduce its deficit (and hence its contribution to domestic demand), then by definition (given the identities) the other two sectors will have to pick up the slack. Given that it is unlikely that the southern private sector will have the confidence in the near future to start investing (nor the available credit), the only mechanism by which the aggregate demand circle will be squared is either the suppression of imports through the drop in household income, or by austerity failing to cut public sector deficits as government revenue chases public spending down. If the private sector had perfect price flexibility it would have the incentives (and ability) for rapid adjustment – but high levels of regulation and the pervasive public sector are likely to make such adjustment painfully slow.

This analysis implies that current policy will be able to solve the euro zone crisis only by very prolonged recession and deflation in the southern states. Even if this policy succeeds in balancing trade flows, the

---

14 By definition, for all countries: public sector deficit = private sector net saving + trade deficit. Note that the exact descriptions and the signs are important for the identity to apply.

residents of the southern states will be left with large, and probably unaffordable, debts in undeflated euros. It is difficult to see how this can be resolved, and prosperity restored, without default on government debt.

Hence the prescription for a break-up is, in my opinion, the best hope for a resumption of prosperity in Europe. It will not happen through the choice of the euro zone elite. It might happen though *force majeure* of some description. If it does, then that break-up will have to be very carefully planned along the lines suggested in this chapter.

8 WHERE SHOULD THE EURO ZONE 'CLUB' GO FROM HERE? HOW A RETURN TO CREDIBLE AND ENFORCEABLE RULES WILL SUSTAIN THE MONETARY UNION

Bodo Herzog[1] and Katja Hengstermann

Sustained economic governance: back to the roots!

The European Monetary Union (EMU) is certainly in a crisis. Without doubt, the recent rescue plans and packages were necessary to stabilise the euro area and the financial markets in the short run (Bundesbank, 2011). It remains questionable, however, whether this rescue path will lead to a sustained framework of economic governance. There is a huge danger that EMU will follow the wrong path – i.e. a short-run rescue philosophy (Economist, 2011). We argue that the consequences of following the current short-term policy will lead to a future break-up. Therefore, we propose an effective rule-based agenda which can lead the euro out of this mess by returning to more credible and enforceable rules. Learning the lessons from the sovereign debt crisis and identifying the failures that allowed the crisis to emerge are essential to build a new economic governance framework.

The current rescue philosophy of helping the indebted countries by providing guarantees on the one hand and demanding strict austerity on the other hand is appropriate only as a short-term stabilisation measure. This rescue strategy does not solve the structural problems and improper incentives of fiscal policy in the EMU in the long run. There is a substantial danger that policymakers will follow the wrong path because of so-called 'political path dependency'. This policy response

1   The authors are grateful to the two anonymous referees for excellent comments and suggestions. We are responsible for all remaining errors.

might put the whole EMU at risk by creating even more moral hazard and free-riding. A solution to the structural problems requires an answer to the question of why the EMU ended up in this mess.

The frequency of new stabilisation packages for Greece and other countries illustrates that the EMU is at a crossroads. The past and current problems are the existence of a weak and non-credible economic governance framework as well as the insufficient enforcement mechanism of existing rules in respect of fiscal discipline. Since the foundation of the EMU in 1999, there have hardly been any officially defined consequences where countries violate the fiscal rules. Strengthening economic governance in the form of ensuring fiscal discipline through strict conditionality is necessary to sustain the EMU's existence (Salines et al., 2011). The recently proposed six-pack and fiscal compact, however, will not be able to tackle all existing structural problems today and in the future (Herzog, 2011, 2012a).

A consensus exists that a sound framework for governance is a prerequisite for successful and sustainable fiscal policies in the EMU (Schuknecht et al., 2011). Hence, a sustainable economic governance framework needs two arms. Firstly, it needs pre-emptive and depoliticised enforcement mechanisms. Secondly, it needs immediate and tough consequences for countries that are not complying with predefined fiscal rules. In the past three years, the European economic governance framework has changed owing to the developments of the European Financial Stability Facility (EFSF) and the European Stability Mechanism (ESM). Despite the strict conditionality of the EFSF and ESM, there is neither an agreement on austerity measures, nor an answer as to how to handle countries that are not complying with the rules. There is no doubt, from a theoretical point of view, that both rescue facilities have led to even fewer incentives to countries to bear the consequences of their own fiscal policy decisions.[2] This will further enforce negative externalities

---

2   Under the ESM, countries pay lower interest rates than under the EFSF and, of course, than in the market. Furthermore, the ECB undertakes outright monetary transactions (OMTs) and thus buys an unlimited number of government bonds if market interest rates are still unsustainable under the ESM grants (ECB, 6 September 2012).

and moral hazard in the European economic governance framework. Thus, a new balance between emergency programmes, fiscal discipline and *ultima ratio* sanctions must be established. Since the first reform of the Stability and Growth Pact (SGP) in 2005, there has been demand for more automatic and independent enforcements in the form of sovereignty limitations when fiscal rules are violated. In this vein we propose a new rule-based framework to sustain the EMU in the long run.

EMU's performance and a theory of optimal rules

Ever since the Maastricht Treaty and the proposal to establish a currency union in the early 1990s, there has been academic discussion about effective fiscal rules. In addition, there was, and still is, a lively debate about the lessons learned from the two rounds of reforms, in 2003–05 and 2010/11, of the SGP. Despite the knowledge of failed historical monetary unions over more than a hundred years (Theurl, 1992), we argue that a credible and enforceable economic governance framework based on market rules is realistic and will be effective. Experience generated by the analysis of past failures enables us to understand the key requirements of a sound rule-based agenda: credible preconditions and enforceable rules with safeguards.

There are different theoretical approaches to analyse properties of a sustainable economic governance framework in EMU. We will focus on a rational choice and institutional economic approach which reflects the two dilemmas in the euro area. A supranational monetary union requires a framework for seventeen completely different and independent members which are linked by interdependent fiscal policies. The effective combination of these interdependent fiscal policies with the independent central bank is supposed to ensure price stability and financial stability.

This constellation is comparable with a collective action dilemma recognised as Arrow's Impossibility Theorem (Arrow, 1951). According to the theorem, this dilemma can be tackled either by creating a hierarchy (i.e. centralisation or dictatorship) or by introducing consistent rules via a market mechanism (i.e. decentralisation). Every government and country faces this dilemma in some policy areas, and most of the Western economies solve it with the second approach: i.e. the implementation of a national constitution which automatically enforces certain principles regardless of political expedience. These rules are known in advance and independently enforced. The first option, a European dictatorship, requires a political union with a supranational budget managed by a finance minister. This is not in place right now and will not be in place in the near future. The second option entails a market environment with a consistent rule-based framework. This is an accessible and realistic option in a supranational monetary union because it combines consistent rules and market forces with effective incentives. A national version of this kind of environment already exists in industrialised countries around the globe. The challenge in a currency union is the design of appropriate fiscal rules that can be applied in a supranational context and which relate to existing national rules.

Herzog (2004a, 2012a) argues that the above-mentioned second option, a rule-based economic governance agenda based on a market approach, is a realistic solution for the current and future EMU. This is not only the best tactic for promoting economic efficiency, but also the most suitable option owing to European society's reluctance to countenance European integration and the recent constitutional court judgement in Germany against the development of a European state. Hence, tackling the fiscal–monetary interaction problem requires an effective rule-based framework (Dixit and Lambertini, 2003; Beetsma and Bovenberg, 2000; Herzog, 2004a) that is enforceable. Moreover, the well-known problem of market failures, such as the lack of provision of public goods (in this case economic, financial and price stability) in a monetary union, immediately signals the need for effective institutions and rules necessary for markets to work efficiently. No effective institutions or rules have been in place in the history of monetary union so far, however. Consequently, today's failing of EMU rules is not a market failure, but rather a policy or state failure (Coase, 1960).

Another theoretical starting point for analysing this problem is game theory. If one member state cheats or rejects cooperation with the fiscal rules and gets away with it, other member states will be encouraged to disobey the rules as well. This will unravel the economic governance framework completely. Theoretically this prisoner's dilemma leads to a vicious circle and a loss of confidence from the outside world. The consequences are higher interest rates and an eventual collapse of the euro area.

Again, this is a problem in a supranational monetary union because of inadequate political institutions. Partisan control over fiscal policy usually leads to deficits caused by incentives to overspend (Alesina and Tabellini, 1987; Nordhaus, 1975). Therefore, political agents do not internalise the social costs of debt policy within, and especially across, countries. Overspending is even more critical and amplified in a monetary union owing to fiscal–monetary interactions and further incentives to free-ride in fiscal matters (Dixit and Lambertini, 2003; Beetsma and Bovenberg, 1999, 2003; Beetsma and Uhlig, 1999). Even within a nation-state, politicians have an incentive to overspend. If they are able to ensure that other countries bear the costs of some of that overspending, however, the incentives are even stronger.

The case of Greece has empirically illustrated this effect. The problem is not just apparent in south European states, however: Standard & Poor's recent announcements of downgrades of countries such as France owing to their relatively high deficits and debt levels illustrate that markets are acutely aware of the problem of unsound public finances in Europe more generally.[3] Countries such as Britain and France show no political commitment to a constitutional debt rule, such as exists in Germany and more recently in Spain. The German 'debt brake' works effectively and enhances the credibility of public finances as the

---

3   Including in Britain, where the issue of imposing costs of deficits on euro zone countries does not arise.

market response has shown during the sovereign debt crisis. Lack of political will and flawed rule design in the EMU due to political horse-trading, however, initially lead to the socialisation of debts, state failure and then the failure of the market itself.

Creating sustainable rules for EMU

The theoretical discussion above provides a basis from which to discuss the practical criteria of an effective rule-based framework for EMU. Kopits and Szymanski (1998) develop characteristics for an efficient and smart rule-based fiscal policy agenda. Following this approach, we provide our assessment of the old and new fiscal rules in the EMU (see Table 3). We use domestic and European data relating to the strictness, objectives and enforcement of fiscal rules. Evaluating the gathered information and categorising it into a ranking-sheet results in our judgement of the twelve characteristics. The table's last column represents an evaluation of the national constitutional debt rule in Germany.

Even if reforms are moving in the right direction, the assessment shows that the old as well as the new economic governance are insufficient in enhancing enforcement and long-run sustainability. Moreover, Table 3 shows the problem of path-dependency, because there is only an incremental change of institutional rules from the pre-existing highly inadequate position. The lack of profound institutional change or a new 'big-bang' solution is part of the crisis of confidence. There is anecdotal evidence that only the close connection of EMU rules to constitutional debt rules on a national level enhances long-run stability in a currency union.

The heterogeneous character of the different EMU members obviously complicates the design and implementation of appropriate fiscal rules. National sovereignty and subsidiarity concerns have to be respected. The rules of member states, however, must be compatible with the goal of a stable EMU if it is to be sustainable. The trade-off between national sovereignty and appropriate rules for a stable EMU requires a clever balance. For example, the growing interaction between

Table 3 **Criteria and assessment of fiscal rules in EMU**

No. criteria	Assessment of economic governance		
	Old EMU rules	New EMU rules (fiscal compact + six-pack)	Constitutional debt-rule (Germany)
1 Well-defined and consistent	+	++	++
2 Simple and easily verifiable	++	+	o
3 Transparency	+	o	o
4 Flexibility, i.e. temporary country specific adjustments	+	+	++
5 Credibility	–	–	+
6 Preemptive mechanism	–	o	+
7 Avoiding pro-cyclical behaviour	o	+	++
8 Encourage long-run sustainability and solvency	–	o	+
9 Automatic or independent enforcement	–	–	–
10 Compliance	–	?	?
11 Credible sanctions on root causes	–	–	+
12 Linkage to national debt rules	–	+	

++ = excellent, + = good, o = satisfactory, – = insufficient.

monetary policy and the fiscal problems of nation-states automatically aggravates the primary goal of price stability (Art. 105, EU Treaty) and thus provokes moral hazard in public finance. In trying to achieve the balance, we will focus on two key aspects in the assessment of appropriate EMU rules: the encouragement of long-run fiscal sustainability and weak enforcement.

The Stability and Growth Pact does not encourage long-run sustainability and credible fiscal consolidation, especially when that can be achieved at lower cost during economic upswings. This is important. Restraining the growth of national debts may be easier for individual nation-states in better economic times, but there is no incentive for such restraint and no pressure from other member states because there is little obvious short-term damage to EMU until a crisis hits. Enforceable rules are therefore needed – and not just at crisis time. This illustrates the first constructional defect. The two regulations 1446/97 and 1447/97 of the SGP explicitly state that the 'excessive deficit procedure' is triggered only if a country violates the 3 per cent deficit-to-GDP and not the 60 per cent debt-to-GDP threshold. Even the reform of the SGP in 2005 did not tackle this obvious gap.

The paradoxical and unjustified overemphasis on deficits, rather than on long-run debt levels, is explained in terms of a political economic argument. A deficit limit is easier to control than sustainable debt levels. The calculation of primary deficits and the distinction between explicit and implicit debt are, however, tricky.

The absence of a long-run objective and the narrow focus on the deficit undermined the credibility of the economic governance framework and impaired long-run sustainability in several EU countries. The triggering mechanism and narrow focus on government deficit within the SGP were also the reasons why Ireland did not even appear on the radar screen as a potential problem. The existing Stability and Growth Pact has overseen both the accumulation and the impact of private deficits and debt levels across countries in the EMU. In addition, there was and still is no mechanism in place to handle the divergence in current account imbalances (or competitiveness) in the euro area.[4] Consequently, the SGP has failed to promote credibility and sustainability in the euro area's public finances. The new fiscal compact and the six-pack partly improve this problem (Herzog, 2012b). It is insufficient, however, to only establish such an economic governance framework. The key is not its design and establishment but an automatic or independent enforcement of the rules.

---

4   Some argue that labour mobility does the job in a monetary union with fixed nominal exchange rates. Empirical evidence suggests, however, that this is only true in the long run (Puhani, 2001). Moreover, labour mobility is far too low to smooth the huge imbalances in the euro area (De Grauwe and Vanhaverbeke, 1993).

The lack of enforcement of rules

As has been discussed, the Achilles heel of the Stability and Growth Pact is its weak enforcement of inadequate provisions, together with a non-existent pre-emptive function. The lack of political willingness to enforce those rules that do exist and the absence of incentives discourages compliance (ECB, 2008).

Firstly, the initiation of the pact's procedure always needed the backing of the Commissioners before any procedural steps could be taken. Secondly, a qualified majority was then required in the ECOFIN Council in order to approve further steps. Euro zone member states that 'sinned' retained the right to vote and needed only a few other countries to block the decision-making process of the Stability and Growth Pact. As long as both sound and unsound countries are part of the ECOFIN Council and are able to decide fiscal policy measures together, EMU's economic governance is doomed to fail. From a rational perspective it would not make sense for a financially unsound country to encourage the punishment of member states breaching the 3 per cent deficit limit if it could be the next one violating the threshold. This is a constructional defect of the decision-making rule and it prevents a credible enforcement of the regulations. When Germany and France, among others, breached the deficit threshold in 2003 and 2004, the ECOFIN Council could not even agree on sending a blue letter (i.e. an early warning) to these countries to remind them of their duties.

The current enforcement mechanism ensures that member states do not internalise the potential costs of deficit and debt accumulation caused by their own policies. This is a well-known problem from the experience of historical monetary unions. Bordo and Lonung (1999) conclude that the cause of the collapse of past monetary unions – such as the Latin Monetary Union from 1914 to 1927 and the Scandinavian monetary union from 1914 to 1924 – was mainly driven by political developments and bad institutional rules. In both cases the dissolution was determined by fiscal policy problems as a consequence of high debt accumulation during World War I. To tackle the root of the problem, we have to go back to a decision-making mechanism that is independent of the offending countries when there are policy failures in those countries. In 1995, the founding father of the Stability and Growth Pact, the former German finance minister Dr Theo Waigel, proposed a completely automatic sanction procedure. At that point in time it was too far-reaching from a political point of view. Today we argue that the time has come for a temporary sovereignty loss in case of sustained violation of the rules to which euro members commit themselves.

The lack of enforcement of rules, of course, causes a compliance problem. Since the onset of EMU, there have been more than sixty breaches of the SGP but none triggered any consequences. Even the first litmus test of a rigorous implementation of the Stability and Growth Pact failed. In autumn 2003, France and Germany, among others, blocked the strict implementation of the pact by colluding in order to reject the Commission's recommendation to move a step further in the sanction procedure. Indeed, the EU Commission was forced by the policymakers in 2005 to propose a reform which would introduce yet greater discretion, leniency, flexibility and political influence into the procedure. A second famous example is the treatment of Greece. Since 2000, Greece has had an annual deficit above 3 per cent of GDP according to ECB data. The first excessive deficit procedure was launched in 2004, however, when the government deficit was 7.9 per cent of GDP.[5] In 2007, the European Commission closed the procedure because they forecast a deficit of 2.9 per cent of GDP, though this turned out to be 6.8 per cent. The debt level in 2007 was forecast to be 97.5 per cent of GDP (it turned out to be 107.4 per cent), well above the reference value of 60 per cent of GDP. Both the EU Commission and the ECOFIN Council failed owing to time lags, misreporting and political unwillingness. Hellwig (2011: 3)

---

5   Some critics argue that the Stability Pact is pro-cyclical and rigid. This is absolutely wrong because the idea of the pact is to provide a pre-emptive mechanism before it leads to pro-cyclicality. The weak enforcement counteracted this idea, however, and led to pro-cyclical effects in the end. Moreover, if countries act in accordance with the pact and adjust the budget close to balance in good times, they have had no or almost no problems with the 3 per cent deficit limit in bad times, as Luxembourg, Estonia or Germany illustrate.

correctly concluded: 'The lack of credibility of the Stability and Growth Pact was identified as a problem [long before]. Therefore it seemed likely that at some point over the medium run, we would come across a problem like the one that Greece has posed over the last year.' Since the SGP reform discussion in 2005, economists have proposed more than a hundred improved alternatives (Fisher et al., 2006). There was still no political will for reform, however.

The phenomenon of non-compliance is a well-known general problem. A few years back Inman (1996) provided an analysis of this problem for the US states. He suggests that, once a rule is established, a mechanism is needed to ensure compliance. Even the new EMU rules, however, developed post-crisis, are insufficient to establish a sound framework with a high level of compliance. In particular, there is closed and partisan enforcement.

More positively, policymakers in some countries have agreed to complement the economic governance framework with constitutional debt rules. Even this will not be effective, however, because there are no links between these new national and supranational rules and there are no incentives to internalise the costs of domestic policies. An example of the former problem is constitutional debt rules that have been adopted in Spain. While welcome, they have been developed in Spain to deal with credibility problems mainly within the Spanish political system itself. If Spain decided to change those rules, it could do so because they do not relate to the supranational system of governance of the euro zone. Again, rules do exist but, because they do not emanate from the EMU institutions, they cannot be enforced by those institutions.

Moreover, European institutions do not analyse and take action over current account imbalances or inflation and growth differentials within the currency union. This is illustrated by the problems that arose in the financial crisis. Financial markets are international but their regulation is still national. It is said that 'banks are international in life, but national in death' (Goodhart, 2009). But this is definitely not true in a monetary union, nor perhaps more generally in an interconnected world. In the case of Ireland, we have learned that the costs of bank bailouts are not just born by Irish taxpayers, but by all European taxpayers – especially those in countries participating in EMU. This illustrates the need for a European rule-based framework in terms of economic and financial regulation and supervision.

Furthermore, the lack of nominal exchange rate movements has destroyed the international competitiveness of important industries in some EU countries. Usually the loss of competitiveness affects the nominal exchange rate but, in a monetary union with irrevocable fixed nominal exchange rates, that mechanism does not work. Eichengreen and Hausmann (1999) have shown that, when lenders distrust governments and refuse to lend in a given country's currency, it will devalue. This would have happened to Greece and Portugal if they had retained their own currency. Indeed, given their lack of fiscal discipline, they would have struggled to borrow in their own currencies in the first place. In the improper EMU framework, markets have learned quickly how to game the rules by lending to governments with inappropriate fiscal policies, knowing that their debts are implicitly guaranteed by others.

Now it's time to learn the lessons and adapt the unsuitable strategy in the euro zone. The almost non-existent economic governance in the past ten years and the recent rescue programmes have taken EMU on the wrong path. This has put all national governments and the EMU at risk. To resolve the current crisis, we have to look for smart solutions and innovative institutional rules which are enforced *ex post* and known to be enforceable *ex ante*. Economically, I would argue that the euro will be beneficial and necessary to tackle the challenges in a world of freer trade and capital movements and in an ageing society (Mongelli, 2008; European Commission, 2011). However, to maintain this monetary union, policymakers must design credible and enforceable rules.

Enforcing enforceable rules

The European Union's policymakers are still far from finding the right way out of the sovereign debt crisis towards a long-run sustainable monetary union. But there is a solution and, after implementing the new rules, the EMU will no longer be endangered.

In this section we will make proposals that will lead to stability within EMU. There are two options. Neither option works, however, without re-establishing and enhancing the credibility of the existing framework. *Option A* (hierarchy) is a fundamental change to the existing policy framework. This option would insist that EMU member states abandon a substantial part of their national sovereignty over fiscal policy. This would require immediate and fundamental legal changes at the European and national levels. The judgment by the constitutional court in Germany has partly eliminated this option for the near future (Bundesverfassungsgericht, 2011). Of course, there is an ongoing delegation of fiscal competences; the key fiscal responsibilities, however, remain on the national level, and they are even being strengthened in the domestic context. For instance, the German constitutional court has also strengthened the rights and veto power of the German parliament significantly (Bundesverfassungsgericht, 2012). Since *Option A* is complex and lacks 'real' political interest as well as support, a European state is currently not a realistic option.

Option B (decentralisation) and an effective rule-based framework aligned with market forces and consistent institutional incentives is more realistic. This will strengthen the fiscal incentives to maintain sound finances within the current framework. *Option B* requires a return to and an enhancement of the fundamental principles of a monetary union. Obviously it is also a 'more European' option (Salines et al., 2011). The following list summarises crucial elements:

- Each member state has to bear the consequences of its own fiscal policy decisions.
- Market interest rates have to serve as a disciplining mechanism in the case of unsound debt policy.
- Pre-emptive and automatic enforcement mechanisms have to support compliance with rules.

- Mechanisms have to smooth differentials between growth rates, inflation rates and current account balances.
- *Ultima ratio* punishment options have to handle notoriously unsound countries.

The key philosophy of *Option B* is that countries bear full responsibility for their own policy actions in combination with a rule-based framework. Consequently, we have to go back to a strict no-bailout clause in Article 125 of the Treaty on the Functioning of the European Union (TFEU). In the same vein, the European Central Bank (ECB) must go back to its primary objective of price stability and must abide by the prohibition of monetary financing (Articles 105 and 123, TFEU). In addition, *Option B* requires a full rethinking and establishment of a supranational economic governance mechanism which is able to tackle the divergence of current accounts and macroeconomic differentials in the euro zone. Undeniably, this mechanism has to be backed by market forces and incentives. The precise make-up of such a toolbox is an issue for further research. We have in mind, however, the use of target functions that are already well known in monetary policy and their application to fiscal and economic policy issues with a solid democratic backing. These target functions define certain target levels and any deviation from targets will almost automatically lead to adjustments.

Such a rule-based framework together with pressure from financial markets would lead to the pre-emptive disciplining of unsound fiscal and economic policy. Pre-emptive warning mechanisms and well-designed fiscal rules are an essential ingredient of successful consolidation according to Holm-Hadulla et al. (2011). In addition, a recent empirical study on the euro area by Escolano et al. (2012) finds that fiscal decentralisation and strict fiscal rules on the supranational and federal level have been associated with better fiscal performance. The basic idea behind these proposals is that the current rule-based approach is not dead (Issing, 2011; Weidmann, 2011) but that weak enforcement, the lack of pre-emptive incentives to encourage sound

Figure 16 **Fiscal Rule Index* and deficit performance, 2009**

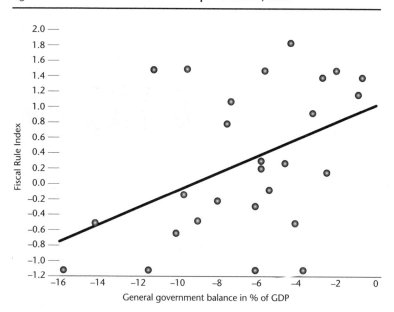

*The Fiscal Rule Index (FRI) is provided by the EU Commission. Its calculation is based on the countries'
information on (i) the statutory base of the rule; (ii) room for setting or revising its objectives; (iii) the body
in charge of monitoring respect for and enforcement of the rule; (iv) the enforcement mechanisms relating
to the rule; and (v) the media visibility of the rule.
Sources: Eurostat, EU Commission, own calculations

public finances and the political discretion in EMU's economic governance are the problems.

A bivariate regression of public deficits and the strictness of fiscal
rules of individual countries show how better fiscal rules are related to
lower deficits in the EU (Figure 16). The relationship is robust despite
the low R-square which is due to the exclusion of major macroeconomic
variables, such as taxes, expenditures, debt levels and the business cycle
position.

Apart from the institutional weaknesses the potential for macroeconomic divergence was not taken into account in the existing economic
governance framework. The dramatic divergence between unit labour

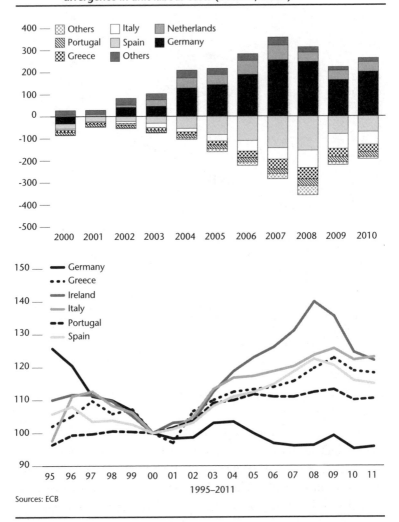

Figure 17 **EMU's current account imbalances (top, € billion) and divergence in unit labour costs (bottom, index)**

Sources: ECB

costs and current account imbalances is just one issue. Figure 17 shows that no mechanism or warning sign has appeared that was acted upon by the ECB despite the evident divergence. We therefore need new mechanisms that internalise the costs of such macroeconomic differentials within the euro zone.

Because there is no permanent loss of sovereignty in *Option B*, a consistent rule-based agenda combined with market forces is necessary to provide discipline. The timing of the reform steps and policy changes is critical for regaining stability within EMU. The ways in which economic governance must be strengthened and extended in several dimensions are outlined below.

Proposal 1: Define ex ante *conditionalities for all EMU member states*

The major underlying policy problem of the rescue packages during the sovereign debt financial crises is moral hazard. To tackle this problem we need consistent incentives towards sound public finances. Therefore, we propose an irrevocable return to the initial incentive structure without exceptions. In order to be a member of EMU, the country must fulfil all stated criteria at the beginning and regularly thereafter. We call this '*ex ante* conditionalities'. These are mandatory conditions for all participating countries made up of (1) sound public finances (i.e. a balanced budget in the medium term), (2) a conservative wage policy and (3) continued economic reforms to enhance growth and competitiveness. In the end, we propose a far more comprehensive and exclusive rule-based framework. A violation of any of these criteria will immediately be identified and/or corrected or sanctioned – similar to mechanisms proposed in relation to austerity packages today.

The current approach leads to tough austerity conditionalities for highly indebted countries after the crisis. This is too late. From the beginning, each country has benefited from EMU without following the necessary rules. Therefore, the existing governance framework sets the wrong incentive at the wrong time. We must make the conditionality of EMU membership *ex ante* and permanent. This strict and irrevocable condition will be effective and reduce pro-cyclicality. Successful budget consolidation has to start in economically good times and requires credible institutional incentives. For the sanctions to be credible, however, EMU cannot be a one-way street. Membership of EMU requires continual fiscal discipline. If a country fails to perform, it will be punished as discussed in the further proposals below.

Proposal 2: Reform the Stability and Growth Pact

The Stability and Growth Pact needs to be reformed in the following way:

1. By introducing immediate sanctions if the deficit threshold, the debt threshold or the goal of a balanced budget in the medium term is violated.
2. By improving the enforcement either with an automatic or a vote-and-reputation mechanism.

These objectives can be reached by introducing an independent fiscal council or an (almost) automatic enforcement mechanism. An independent fiscal council should be structured in a way similar to the Swedish Fiscal Policy Council (Calmfors, 2010) or the German Council of Economic Experts, according to a proposal by the ECB (2010). The council consists of five or more independent members who are academics who possess expert knowledge in economics and public finance. Alternatively, if there is no agreement to an independent fiscal council, we suggest an automatic enforcement or an 'intelligent voting mechanism' within the Stability and Growth Pact. This voting mechanism involves the loss of voting power in the excessive deficit procedure for all countries with deficits above 3 per cent of national income. This is an immediate and explicit sanction for unsound members of the euro area. Casella (2001) and Herzog (2004b, 2004c) developed such vote-and-reputation mechanisms. The mechanism mainly depends on three factors: the target gap between the excessive deficit and the 3 per cent deficit limit; the frequency of violations; and the time horizon to achieve the balanced budget. These three determinants trigger a gradual reduction in the voting rights of the member states in the ECOFIN Council. In case of sustained policy violation the mechanism leads to a full loss of sovereignty. Such an intrinsic punishment in terms of loss of sovereignty is preferable to the current extrinsic incentives of monetary sanctions (Herzog, 2004a). It is the only mechanism that can establish a smart way for countries to internalise the costs of their policy decisions without centralising fiscal power. Only countries that are behaving in line with the founding principles of the euro will have full sovereignty and voting power, whereas those which are not – and which are imposing costs on others owing to their fiscal profligacy – will lose voting power. Economically, one could see such a vote-and-reputation mechanism as an insurance premium for the sound countries. An automatic mechanism is quite similar to a vote-and-reputation function. The latter is more effective, however, because there is no discretion. From a political point of view, the vote-and-reputation function is therefore the most realistic and effective option in the near future.

The EMU's rule-based framework will not work as long as the policymakers, whose job it is to enforce the rules, are motivated by economic and political incentives to neglect to do so. A transparent incentive system will enhance the credibility of economic governance in the future because every country will know in advance that a violation triggers a significant loss of sovereignty.

Proposal 3: Introduce enforcement measures leading to a loss of sovereignty or a principle of exclusion in the case of unsound fiscal policy

Owing to the specific constellation of fiscal–monetary interaction and the emergency programmes of the European Financial Stability Facility and later on the European Stability Mechanism other incentives towards sound fiscal policy are needed. Firstly, we recommend a strictly enforceable and more credible no-bailout clause in line with Article 125 of the EU

Treaty. This includes that the ECB must follow its legal mandate of price stability (Article 105, EU Treaty) and reject implicit monetary financing (Aliber, 2012). The acceptance of collateral bonds for open market operations by the ECB should depend on the ECB's independent assessment of the sustainability of countries' public finances in order to achieve the target of price stability. This assessment might range from limited access to repo operations through the use of substantial haircuts through to the refusal of government bonds issued by notoriously unsound countries that breach the pact. Of course, the new fiscal and economic rules cannot avoid unforeseen shocks or banking crises, which is why we need emergency measures. Both monetary and fiscal policy, however, should act independently of each other within this mandate. Secondly, the European Stability Mechanism should only be allowed to serve as lender of last resort for member states in very special cases and with even stricter austerity conditions which avoid an enduring interest rate subsidy. In other words, we need to return to realistic market interest rates that reflect the idiosyncratic risks – including credit risks – of euro-denominated bonds.

In addition, we propose that the European Stability Mechanism should focus on countries in trouble owing to massive exogenous shocks, unforeseen and significant market reversals or catastrophes. It should be a temporary mechanism and not a bailout fund for inherently unsound governments. Countries with unsustainable public budgets or countries which have not complied with the fiscal rules for several years should have access only if they give up their full sovereignty. Also, to sustain the long-run stability of the monetary union, we propose an *ultima ratio* sanction for unsound states. Countries violating fiscal rules for more than three or four years in a row would then lose full fiscal sovereignty and could continue use of the euro only with no participation in its governance mechanisms. Alternatively, they would have to leave EMU. After fulfilling the *ex ante* conditionalities, the country would either regain national sovereignty, or, in case of exclusion, be given the option to rejoin the governance mechanisms of EMU under certain defined conditions.

Proposal 4: Democratise European Union economic governance

The new rules and institutions for fiscal policy must serve the purpose of democratising European economic governance. Those means will serve each national citizen best by maintaining a national policy system and integrating supranational coordination only in special cases. If a country fails to consolidate the public budget, however, or to enhance domestic competitiveness, the supranational level should take more and more responsibility for this specific country. In normal times, we recommend an environment in which fiscal policy is applied effectively at the national level to promote national needs (Oates, 1972, 1999). That way it will enhance the welfare of domestic and neighbouring countries most effectively. It is important that fiscally sound countries can decide about the use of their taxpayers' money and the new rules and principles must serve the purpose of European citizens by making our institutions more democratic.

The old rule-based framework was not complete, consistent or credible. Thus, an effective economic governance agenda will offer the opportunity to be successful in the long run. As with a football match, only with an effective referee can the best players show their real talent. Well-designed and enforced rules prevent countries from 'playing rough' and unfairly and support fair play by those countries which abide by the rules that are necessary for monetary union to work.

Conclusion

European Monetary Union will not fail and the integration process will not be reversed if policymakers return to credible, strict, consistent and enforceable rules. Our proposed mechanism will create a well-founded EMU in the long run. Moreover, policymakers have to learn that fiscal policy in a monetary union requires continual hard work.

First and foremost we have to remove the arbitrariness of fiscal rules and economic governance. Together with the democratisation of European economic governance we would propose a more stable and sustainable EMU. The lesson from the crisis is not that the EU should become a political union but that stable and enforceable rules should be developed and that these rules need to be enforced in better economic times.

The euro zone needs to refine, extend and enhance existing rules as well as complement these rules and institutions with better enforcement procedures, pre-emptive incentives and intelligent sanctions. Of course, an effective economic governance framework restricts the room for manoeuvre, but market forces also do the same in the sense that those taking economic decisions have to bear the consequences of those decisions rather than impose the consequences on others. Such an enforceable rules framework is the price that needs to be paid for the benefits of a currency union. We must design the rules in such a way that they serve the people best and promote long-term growth.

References

Alesina, A. and G. Tabellini (1987), 'Rules and discretion with noncoordinated monetary and fiscal policies', *Economic Inquiry*, 25(4): 619–30.

Aliber, R. Z. (2012), *Your Money and Your Life*, Palo Alto, CA: Stanford University Press.

Arrow, K. J. (1951), *Social Choice and Individual Values*, New York: Wiley.

Beetsma, R. M. W. J. and A. L. Bovenberg (1999), 'Does monetary unification lead to excessive debt accumulation?', *Journal of Public Economics*, 74(3): 299–325.

Beetsma, R. M. W. J. and A. L. Bovenberg (2000), 'Designing fiscal and monetary institutions for a monetary union', *Public Choice*, 102(3/4): 247–69.

Beetsma, R. M. W. J. and A. L. Bovenberg (2003), 'Strategic debt accumulation in a heterogeneous monetary union', *European Journal of Political Economy*, 19(1): 1–15.

Beetsma, R. M. W. J. and H. Uhlig (1999), 'An analysis of the Stability and Growth Pact', *Economic Journal*, 109(458): 546–71.

Bordo, M. D. and L. Lonung (1999), 'The future of EMU: what does the history of monetary unions tell us?', NBER Working Paper no. 7365.

Bundesbank (2011), *Monatsberichte*, Frankfurt.

Bundesverfassungsgericht (2011), *Euro-Rettungsschirm*, 7 September.

Bundesverfassungsgericht (2012), *ESM-Urteil*, 12 September.

Calmfors, L. (2010), 'The Swedish Fiscal Policy Council – experiences and lessons', paper presented at the Conference on Independent Fiscal Institutions, Budapest, 18/19 March.

Casella, A. (2001), 'Market mechanisms for policy decisions: tools for the European Union', *European Economic Review*, 45: 995–1006.

Coase, R. H. (1960), 'The problem of social cost', *Journal of Law and Economics*, 3: 1–44.

De Grauwe, P. and W. Vanhaverbeke (1993), 'Is Europe an optimum currency area? Evidence from regional data', in P. R. Masson and M. P. Taylor (eds), *Policy Issues in the Operation of Currency Unions*, Cambridge: Cambridge University Press.

Dixit, A. and L. Lambertini (2003), 'Symbiosis of monetary and fiscal policies in a monetary union', *Journal of International Economics*, 60(2): 235–47.

ECB (2008), 'Ten years of the Stability and Growth Pact', *Monthly Bulletin*, Frankfurt, October.

ECB (2009), 'New survey evidence on wage setting in Europe', *Monthly Bulletin*, Frankfurt, February, pp. 69–83.

ECB (2010), 'Reinforcing economic governance in the euro area', Frankfurt, June.

ECB (2011), 'Determinants of inflation differentials in the euro area', *Monthly Bulletin*, Frankfurt, January/February, pp. 40–43.

Economist (2011), 'Europe's currency crisis – how to save the euro', *The Economist*, 17 September.

Eichengreen, B. and R. Hausmann (1999), 'Exchange rates and financial fragility', *Proceedings*, Federal Reserve Bank of Kansas City, pp. 329–68.

Escolano, J. et al. (2012), 'Fiscal performance, institutional design and decentralization in European Union countries', IMF Working Paper no. 12/45.

European Commission (2011), 'Adopting the Euro – who can join and when?', http://ec.europa.eu/economy_finance/euro/adoption/who_can_join/index_en.htm, accessed 12 April 2012.

Fisher, J. et al. (2006), '101 proposals to reform the Stability and Growth Pact. Why so many? A survey', *European Economy*, 267, EU Commission.

Goodhart, C. A. C. (2009), 'Procyclicality and financial regulation', *Banco de España*, 16 (online).

Hellwig, M. (2011), 'Quo vadis, Euroland? European Monetary Union between crisis and reform', MPI Working Paper no. 12.

Herzog, B. (2004a), 'Warum verstoßen vorwiegend die großen EWU-Länder gegen den "Stabilitäts- und Wachstumspakt"?', *Quarterly Journal of Economic Research*, 73(3): 405–17.

Herzog, B. (2004b), 'Fiscal–monetary interaction and the Stability and Growth Pact: focus on: reforming the pact', *SMYE Conference Proceedings*, Warsaw.

Herzog, B. (2004c), 'Modes of economic governance and interaction conflicts: the Stability and Growth Pact and its institutional inconsistencies', in Yiannis A. Stivachtis (ed.), *International Governance and International Security: Issues and Perspectives*, Athens: ATINER.

Herzog, B. (2011), 'Wohin steuert die Europäische Wirtschafts- und Währungsunion', *Positionen*, 19: 7–35, Berlin: Konrad-Adenauer Stiftung.

Herzog, B. (2012a), 'EMU at crossroads', *CESifo Forum*, 4/2011: 23–9.

Herzog, B. (2012b), 'Die Zukunft Europas – Zwischen Regelbindung und Politischer Union: Ökonomische Bewertung der Maßnahmen im Hinblick auf eine "Fiskalunion"', ed. C. Calliess, *E-paper in European Law*, 78: 1–38.

Holm-Hadulla, F., S. Hauptmeier and P. Rother (2012), 'The impact of numerical expenditure rules on budgetary discipline over the cycle', *Applied Economics*, 44(25): 3287–3296.

Inman, R. P. (1996), *Balanced Budget Rules and Public Deficits: Evidence from the U.S. States*, Carnegie-Rochester Conference Series on Public Policy.

Issing, O. (2011), 'Slithering to the wrong kind of union', *Financial Times*, 9 August.

Kopits, G. and G. Szymanski (1998), 'Fiscal policy rules', IMF Occasional Papers no. 162.

Mongelli, F. P. (2008), *European Economic and Monetary Integration and the Optimum Currency Area Theory*, No. 302, Brussels: Directorate General Economic and Monetary Affairs, European Commission, http://ideas.repec.org/s/euf/ecopap.html.

Nordhaus, W. D. (1975), 'The political business cycle', *Review of Economic Studies*, 42: 169–90.

Oates, W. E. (1972), *Fiscal Federalism*, New York: Harcourt Brace Jovanovich.

Oates, W. E. (1999), 'An essay on fiscal federalism', *Journal of Economic Perspectives*, 37(3): 1120–49.

Puhani, P. A. (2001), 'Labour mobility: an adjustment mechanism in Euroland? Empirical evidence for western Germany, France and Italy', *German Economic Review*, 2(2): 127–40.

Salines, M., G. Glöckler, Z. Truchlewski and P. del Favero (2011), 'Beyond the economics of the Euro – analysing the institutional evolution of EMU 1999–2010', ECB Occasional Paper Series no. 127, Frankfurt, September.

Schuknecht, L. et al. (2011), 'The Stability and Growth Pact – crisis and reform', ECB Occasional Paper Series no. 129, Frankfurt, September.

Theurl, T. (1992), 'Eine gemeinsame Währung für Europa: 12 Lehren aus der Geschichte', Vienna: Österreichischer Studien Verlag.

Weidmann, J. (2011), 'Die Krise als Herausforderung für die Währungsunion', *Rede*, 13 September.

9 BACK TO THE FUTURE: A FREE BANKING SOLUTION FOR THE EURO ZONE

Kevin Dowd[1]

Although many still refuse to acknowledge it, the current euro zone crisis is terminal: it is bound to lead to the end of the euro zone as we currently know it and may well destroy the European Union itself by the time it has run its course. This is because the great European federalist 'project' – embodied by the Maastricht Treaty, the European Central Bank and European federalist institutions in general; in effect, the project of building a European United States – was always built on unsound foundations.

Two structural problems in particular stand out. The first is the problem of fiscal moral hazard or inadequate fiscal control – in particular, of countries on the fringe borrowing excessively on the assumption that they could expect to be bailed out if they got themselves into difficulties. The second is the democratic deficit – the fact that federalist institutions are unaccountable and democratic controls very weak.[2] This democratic deficit is itself a reflection of an even deeper problem, i.e. that many of the peoples of Europe never 'bought into' the European federalist project in the first place. Thus, the EU has a legitimation deficit as well. Each of these problems was identified by critics right at its inception, and yet none was ever seriously addressed – let alone solved – by

---

1 The author would like to thank two referees for their helpful comments on an earlier draft.
2 So, for example, in some countries (such as the UK) the electorate were never given a chance to vote on the federalist reforms; in other countries, referenda rejecting them were overridden. A case in point was Denmark in 1992; the electorate rejected the Maastricht Treaty but the Danish government later held a second referendum in which the Danish public were deceived and browbeaten into returning an acceptable 'yes' vote (see Dowd, 1998: 365–6): electorates were therefore free to accept the reforms, but not to reject them.

the arrogant and unaccountable Euro-federalists who drove this project and who now see it unravelling as long-denied economic and political realities finally reassert themselves.

It follows that their usual 'solutions' – more panicked bailouts, more debt issues, more smoke-and-mirrors securitisations, such as the entertainingly misnamed Long-Term Refinancing Operations, the European Financial Stability Facility (EFSF), the European Stability Mechanism (ESM), etc. – will never work and simply put off the day of reckoning. These responses buy time at the cost of making underlying problems worse and merely throw good money after bad.[3]

Similarly, the other 'solution' touted in recent months – of tighter fiscal discipline, boiling down in practice to proposals to allow Germany to control many other countries' fiscal policies – will not work either. Such proposals would greatly aggravate the existing democratic deficit and would make much of Europe into what might politely be described as a German 'sphere of influence' – and never mind the fact that the Germans themselves do not want such power but wish only to limit the costs which they are being expected to bear. The inevitable nationalist reaction to German fiscal control would then rip the EU apart.

At times such as these it is always helpful to step back and think in terms of first principles rather than some hurried quick 'fix' that is likely to fall apart rapidly. One way to do so is to ask what features we would want an ideal system to have.

A list of such features is shown in Table 4; these are contrasted with the corresponding features of the present system. We see that the current system is characterised by: arbitrary politicised monetary policymaking, a tendency to inflation, manipulated interest rates giving rise to asset price bubbles and major misallocation of resources, a highly

---

3   My focus of interest in this article is with the EU, but it is worth noting that the USA shares some but not all of the problems faced by the EU. Its currency is also losing credibility and its fiscal policy is also out of control and unsustainable. The USA does not share the fiscal moral hazard that is tearing the euro zone apart, however, and does not have the 'legitimation' deficit that the EU has.

Table 4 **Current versus ideal monetary and financial systems**

	Current system	Ideal system
Monetary policy	Arbitrary, politicised, policymakers unaccountable	No problem because there is no monetary policy
Inflation	Prone to inflation because there is no limit to money issue	Price level tied to one or more commodities; control against over-issue of money
Interest rates	Manipulated, resulting in bubbles and misallocated resources	Market-determined and stable
Financial stability	Financial system weakened and prone to crisis	Highly stable owing to constraints against over-issue of currency
Sustainability of financial system	Not sustainable owing to short-term focus	Sustainable; long-term focus
Bank corporate governance	Weak	Strong
Risk-taking	Out of control	Reined in; sensible trade-offs
Sustainability of financial system	Weak owing to short-term focus	Sustainable; long-term focus
Accountability	Weak to none*	Strong
Financial regulation	Prudential regulation as per FSA: does not work	Not needed
Cost to taxpayer	Incalculable but certainly large	None
Track record	System collapsing	Very good
Capital regulation, e.g. Basel	Costly and does not work	Not needed as system is healthy and stable

*Current central banks are subject to very limited accountability, at best. In the USA, for example, this is borne out by the Federal Reserve's fierce and largely successful opposition to making itself even auditable. In Europe, the situation is even worse, and even the EU itself has not had its accounts signed off for seventeen years. As for the UK, the Bank of England is subject to parliamentary scrutiny, the obligation to issue open letters if it fails to meet its inflation target, and so on; such accountability mechanisms, however, seem to have had little impact in forcing the Bank to tighten its monetary policy post-2007 in order to meet its statutory inflation obligations, which it has been in practice ignoring since at least 2009.

unstable (and now insolvent) financial system, poor governance structures, out-of-control risk-taking, a short-term focus, no accountability, useless regulatory bodies and a huge cost to the taxpayer.

By contrast, the ideal system is characterised by the opposites: no problematic monetary policy, long-term price stability, control against the over-issue of money, stable market-driven interest rates, a stable financial system, a long-term focus, strong governance, controlled risk-taking, accountability, the absence of useless regulatory bodies and no cost to the taxpayer. And this ideal system *also* has a very good historical track record.

The ideal system is clearly much superior; indeed, it is as different from the current system as it is possible to be. This ideal system is free banking – a truly free market in money and finance.

Historical record of free banking

It is important to appreciate that free banking is not some untested theory. On the contrary, it has a strong historical track record that is usually ignored by most modern economists who take for granted the 'need' for central banks, financial regulation and inconvertible paper currency. In a survey article published twenty years ago, Kurt Schuler (1992a) counts at least sixty historical experiences of free (or nearly) free banking systems. These include cases in Scotland, Ireland, France, Switzerland, Sweden, Australia, New Zealand, parts of the USA during the antebellum period, South America and China. Most if not all these systems had multiple note issuers, branch banking, clearing arrangements between the banks, and high levels of competition and innovation. Currency issues were convertible – often into gold – and were widely accepted and usually long-lasting. There was no central bank, no lender of last resort, no bailout mechanism for banks that got themselves into difficulties and, by modern standards, very limited scope for government intervention. These systems were highly stable and bank crises were relatively rare: when they did occur, such problems were typically centred on one or a small number of weak banks, and bank runs rarely posed systemic threats to the banking system as a whole. Typically, some weak bank would be exposed and run out of business, and its market share would be taken over by stronger rivals. In short, such systems were typically convertible, stable and highly successful.[4]

The most famous such system is that of Scotland, which enjoyed free banking for much of the eighteenth and early nineteenth centuries. The Scottish system was much superior to the contemporary English banking system, which was crippled by the monopoly privileges of the Bank of England and other legal restrictions that left most English banks small, weak and unstable. It is also noteworthy that Scotland was almost untouched by the great English banking crisis of December 1825, which almost destroyed the English banking system and led to a wave of resentment against the Bank of England that almost saw the Bank lose its charter in the years afterwards. Perhaps the most successful of all, however, was the Canadian free banking system, which evolved in the early nineteenth century and lasted until well into the twentieth century – Canada adopted a central bank only in 1934. The Canadian experience of free banking was highly successful and far superior to the much more regulated and less stable systems that predominated south of the Canadian border.[5]

Such systems typically came to an end for one of three reasons. In some countries, governments squeezed out competitive note issue and established monopoly banks to extract seigniorage revenues from the banking system. In others, free banking was ended by some crisis – typically a currency crisis brought on by a war – that led the government to make the currency inconvertible. In other cases, most notably in countries such as Scotland, Canada and Australia, it was ended by a shift in the ideological climate towards a (mistaken) belief in the theoretical superiority of central banking systems.[6]

4　For more on the theory and historical experience of free banking, see, for example, Dowd (1988, 1992, 1996), Horwitz (1992), Selgin (1988), Smith (1936) and White (1984).

5　Schuler (1992b) provides a nice overview of Canadian free banking.

6　In Britain, Scottish free banking was eliminated by the victory of the Currency School

The new systems of central banking and state control that replaced free banking were, however, less stable and more prone to inflation thanks to state or central-bank meddling in the economy. And so, ironically, the earlier superior free market monetary and banking systems were replaced by the inferior statist systems that most modern economists still take for granted.

So how would we establish – or rather re-establish – a free banking system?

Monetary standard

The first requirement is to end current fiat monetary systems and (re-) establish a sound commodity-based monetary standard. This would entail the end of inconvertible paper currency. Henceforth, any paper currency would be redeemable on demand for some appropriate redemption media of a given nominal value. A natural example would be the UK gold standard in the nineteenth century: under this system the pound sterling was defined as a particular amount of gold and a pound note was merely a receipt entitling the owner to claim this amount of gold from the issuer.

Under any commodity standard, currency – banknotes, deposits and other exchange media – would be convertible, and the obligation to maintain convertibility would provide a discipline against the over-issue of currency: any excess currency issue that the public did not want to hold would be returned to the issuer for redemption. By contrast,

---

and the passage of the Bank Charter Act of 1844 – in effect, a historical accident – which abolished the free issue of banknotes. The Scottish banking system remained strong and highly respected for long afterwards, however. Indeed, even into (at least) the 1960s, when I was a child in the north of England, people still trusted Scottish banknotes more than the official legal tender issued by the Bank of England. It is also interesting that the success of the free Scottish system remained inexplicable to the (English) economists who supported central banking in one form or another. A notable example was John Stuart Mill: the best explanation he could come up with was that free banking was a very good thing north of the Tweed but a very bad thing south of it – not the most convincing explanation from one of the greatest minds of the age. See also Smith (1936) and White (1984).

under an inconvertible fiat system there is nothing to contain the over-issue of currency, and any excess issue goes into the broader economy where it distorts prices and disrupts economic activity – not least in the form of damaging boom/bust asset-bubble cycles – and in the long term produces inflation.

To establish a commodity standard, one would need to choose a suitable commodity 'anchor', and the choice of anchor (or, if one prefers, the type of commodity-money standard) would determine the behaviour of the price level over time. Under a gold standard, for example, the nominal price of gold would be fixed and the price level would vary inversely with the relative price of gold against goods and services in general. In effect, the price level would be determined by the factors that equilibrate the market for gold: if demand for gold rose faster than supply, then the relative price of gold would rise and the price level would fall, and vice versa.[7] The gold standard served us well historically and delivered a high degree of long-term price-level stability.[8]

One can also envisage alternatives to gold: systems based on silver, oil, other commodities and even bricks have all been suggested. One could also have systems based on commodity baskets instead of single commodities: these include symmetallism (a basket of fixed amounts of gold and silver) or baskets of other commodities such as those proposed by Marshall (1887) or Friedman in his proposal for a Commodity Reserve Currency (Friedman, 1951). Extensions of such systems include various proposals involving rules to adjust the commodity content of the basket to produce a more stable price level than would be achieved under a gold standard.[9] Such systems are

7   One can also envisage forms of gold standard under which the price of gold is not fixed These have been suggested by Williams (1892) and Friedman (1968), among others.

8   For example, under the gold standard, prices in the UK were much the same in 1914 as they had been almost a century earlier. By comparison, after almost a century of fiat money, the pound today is worth under 1 per cent of what it was worth in 1914. For more on historical gold standards, see, for example, Jastram (2009).

9   The most famous example is Irving Fisher's 'compensated dollar' of 100 years ago (Fisher,

potentially superior to the gold standard but none of them has ever been tested.

Nor is there any need for European countries to agree to a single standard. Different currencies might be based on alternative standards, in which case their exchange rates would fluctuate against each other as the market values of the commodities involved changed: we would then have currency blocs based on different commodity standards.

Abolition of central banking, financial regulation and state support

The second key feature of a free banking system would be the abolition of central banks, financial regulation, legal tender laws[10] and all forms of state support or guarantee, including state deposit insurance, lender of last resort, too big to fail, and other bailouts. Indeed, all state support of any sort to the financial system would be expressly prohibited.

There would no longer be any central bank to govern the banking system, set interest rates, determine monetary policy, influence the price level or credit conditions or otherwise interfere in the economy. Indeed, there would be no monetary policy at all, just the free market. The ending of monetary policy would also put an end to the state using monetary policy to monetise its debt, and the state would no longer have any privileged access to debt markets.

Banks would be free to issue any form of currency they wished subject only to the discipline of the market operating under the rule of law; for their part, the public would be free to use any currency they

---

1913). More recent proposals attempt to achieve price-level stability by means of a monetary rule that aims to stabilise the expected price level using financial instruments (for example, Dowd, 1999).

10 Legal tender laws are unnecessary because historical experience shows that people will willingly accept currency they trust. Historically, legal tender laws have been used to force people to accept currency – typically inconvertible paper currency issued by the state – that they might be reluctant to accept of their own free will.

chose.[11] If any bank got into difficulties, there would be no state support to assist it and it would sink or swim accordingly – classic survival of the fittest. In the absence of deposit insurance or a lender of last resort, banks would also be exposed to the ever-present threat of bank runs. The public would be mindful that their note currency and deposits would be potentially at risk, and they would choose and monitor their banks accordingly: any whiff of trouble and they would be ready to run. Since a bank run could put the bank out of business, bankers would respond with credible measures to reassure depositors. In particular, they would be more conservative in their risk-taking and operate on much lower leverage ratios (i.e. maintain higher capital ratios). The very threat of a run would make banks safer and stronger.

Once in a while, some bank would get itself into difficulties and either be brought into line by market discipline or, *in extremis*, be run out of business.[12] The historical experience of relatively unregulated banking systems, however, is that such bank failures would rarely pose any systemic threat to the banking system; on the contrary, they would strengthen it by weeding out the weak and unfit in a process of financial Darwinism. This would also remind other bankers of the need to maintain their banks' financial health.

There would also be no financial regulation: the only 'regulation' that would be needed is the regulation provided by the law, especially the law of contract and laws governing remedy.[13] There would be no need for

---

11   The freedom to choose their own currency would also extend to the freedom to use foreign currencies (including those issued by foreign central banks) and new currencies (such as Bitcoin).

12   For instance, a bank might over-issue its currency but then experience a loss of reserves through the interbank clearing system, which would ensure that the excess currency was returned to it for redemption. Alternatively, a bank might experience losses on its loan portfolio, the revelation of which would dent public confidence in it and possibly lead to a bank run. In less serious cases, the bank would be able to ride out a run at considerable cost to its public standing, leading perhaps to senior bank officers losing their jobs; in more serious cases, the bank would be unable to survive and the run would force it into bankruptcy.

13   Legal remedies are in themselves badly in need of reform: taking financial institutions to court is extremely expensive and the ombudsman system is essentially a failure. What is

FSA-type prudential regulatory bodies: competition for market share would ensure quality of service and basic standards. Relatedly, there would be no need for capital regulation, as market forces would suffice to keep banks strong, and banks would be free to set their own capital ratios, manage their own financial and liquidity risks, and set their own reserve ratios.[14] Prudential and capital regulatory bodies (including Basel) could then be abolished: these have proved to be almost totally ineffective anyway.[15] Whether we are talking of prudential regulation or capital regulation, experience shows that box-ticking by regulators is no substitute for the discipline provided by free market forces.

Sound accounting standards

Getting the numbers right is the absolute bedrock of sound economic and financial calculation. Traditional accounting standards in the UK were based on the principle that accounts should be prepared prudently and should provide a 'true and fair view' of a company's financial position. The requirement to do this was (and still is) enshrined in UK company law.

Unfortunately, the adoption of International Financial Reporting Standards (IFRS) in 2005 served greatly to undermine UK accounting, especially bank accounting. Central to this is the way in which IFRS attempts to implement 'mark-to-market' accounting: this, however, has created an utter disaster as it encouraged all manner of accounting shenanigans which have only come to light since mid-2011 – such as RBS's now notorious £25 billion 'black hole' (see Armitstead, 2011). Others keep coming to light every few weeks. The bottom line is that

---

needed is reform to allow members of the public quick and inexpensive means of seeking redress.

14 Banks would therefore be free to operate on a fractional reserve basis but would bear the illiquidity risks in doing so. At the same time, there would be no requirement for banks to operate on a fractional reserve basis, and banks operating on a 100 per cent reserve basis would be free to operate.

15 See, for example, Dowd et al. (2011) and Kerr (2011).

banks' accounts can no longer be trusted and the only thing that we can be sure about is that the true situation is (much) worse than it might appear to be.

It is therefore essential to restore sound accounting standards. The UK could do so by returning to traditional Generally Accepted Accounting Practices (GAAP) under existing company law.[16]

Strong governance and extended liability

Another critical element is the restoration of strong governance structures in banking, and the key to this is extended personal liability. The main principle here is to ensure that those who make major decisions are held accountable and made liable for them. Ideally, we should roll back the limited liability statutes which were a major legislative intervention in the mid-nineteenth century that was bitterly opposed by the free marketeers of the time.[17] These statutes created a major moral hazard leading to excessive risk-taking and a weakening of corporate governance. The limited liability or joint-stock corporate form was famously denounced by Adam Smith in the *Wealth of Nations* for exactly this reason.

Failing such a reform, a more limited 'second-best' solution might be to double the liability of bank shareholders (as was the practice in the USA following the introduction of the limited liability privilege) and reinforce the currently existing (but in practice lapsed) unlimited liability of bank directors. Indeed, in a free banking system, banks

---

16 For more on the weaknesses of mark-to-market accounting, see, for example, Dowd and Hutchinson (2010) and Kerr (2011). The weaknesses of IFRS accounting were vividly revealed by Tim Bush and Gordon Kerr, who exposed – among other scandals – the inadequacies of RBS's published accounts, which RBS has now all but admitted. The problems with IFRS led British MP Steve Baker to put a private member's Bill, the Financial Services (Regulation of Derivatives) Bill, before Parliament in early 2011. This Bill proposed that banks be required to prepare accounts under the earlier, pre-IFRS, UK GAAP and in accordance with UK company law. Unfortunately, the Baker Bill never made it to the third reading.

17 A splendid analysis of the impact of this legislation is provided by Campbell and Griffin (2006).

may well adopt unlimited or double liability through choice, as often happened in the USA. Having a mechanism to signal to the market that shareholders had 'skin in the game' was – and would be – extremely important in a free banking system.

An example of an attempt to return to unlimited liability was Steve Baker's second private member's Bill, the Financial Institutions (Reform) Bill 2012, which, among other measures to make bankers behave responsibly, proposed that bank directors be held strictly liable for any bank losses and that they be required to post personal bonds that would be forfeit in the event of any reported bank losses.[18]

Fiscal reform

These reforms would help establish a system that would be much superior to the one we currently have. The historical record also clearly indicates the Achilles heel of any such system, however: this is not because the system has any major inherent weakness as such; rather, the problem is the vulnerability of the banking system and the currency to predation by the state. Traditionally, this predation takes one of two forms: the state pressuring the banking system for subsidised loans to circumvent constraints on 'regular' taxation (and often to fund wars); and simple currency debasement or inflation, which of course is just another but highly destructive form of hidden taxation. Consequently, the long-term security of any free banking system requires fiscal and indeed constitutional reform to protect the system from attack by the state itself.

One proposal sometimes made is the addition of a balanced-budget

---

18 The main problem is that the current system requires that fault be proved, and the bar to establishing fault has risen to the point where it is almost impossible to prove. Hence the proposal in the second Baker Bill to make directors strictly liable: this would remove the need to prove fault and rule out the usual excuses from directors seeking to evade responsibility. This proposal provides a nice incentive for directors to be ultra-careful lest they lose all their personal wealth. As one UK MP said to Mr Baker, 'If your Bill becomes law, then a banker will be apt to wake up in a cold sweat worrying that his daughter might lose her horse.' This is exactly the point.

amendment to the constitution (or the closest one can get to that in countries with no written constitution) in which the government is required to balance its budget over some period. The historical experience with such rules, however, is that governments eventually broke them down: this indicates the need for more radical fiscal reform.

I would therefore suggest something more robust and more far-reaching – namely, that the issue of government debt be prohibited outright *and* that the government be prohibited from issuing any form of financial guarantee or commitment. The former measure would force governments to fund future expenditures properly – and I use the word 'fund' in the correct sense of putting money aside to provide for future financial commitments, as opposed to the current 'pay-as-you-go' system that relies on future tax revenues to pay for commitments made earlier. The latter measure would make it impossible for governments to bail out insolvent financial institutions. Taken together, these measures would also do away with unsound smoke-and-mirrors bailout securitisation scams – the ESM and so on – by which the European authorities currently seek to defy economic and financial reality by kicking the can down the road for others to pick up.

Above all, such rules would impose a stern fiscal discipline and force governments to live within their means: this would put a stop to them writing cheques on future taxpayers. If a government wanted to spend, it would have to finance that spending using current regular (i.e. explicit) taxation without resorting to hidden taxes or passing the cost to future generations – and it would have to make the political case accordingly. The economic pain would be up front and fairly obvious. To further reinforce fiscal discipline, I would also recommend the abolition of progressive income taxation. This would put a stop to politicians promoting policies to one set of voters to be paid for by others. Taxpayers who voted for more spending would then know that they would have to bear the higher tax burden themselves.[19]

---

19 Carswell (2012) makes a compelling case for the abolition of progressive taxation. He also emphasises that it was the introduction of progressive taxation a century ago that opened

In this context, it is also important to note the utter uselessness of current fiscal 'rules' governing euro zone governments. The most egregious examples are the deficit/GDP and debt/GDP rules under the Maastricht Treaty: these stipulate a maximum deficit of 3 per cent of GDP and a maximum debt ceiling of 60 per cent of GDP; they have been blatantly ignored for years and are honoured only in the breach. Such rules lack any credible enforcement mechanism and – to state the obvious – a rule that is not enforced is not in fact a rule at all, but merely hot air.

Unrealistic?

Of course, many people would object that these proposals are 'unrealistic'. This sort of response is usually made by those who think we should tinker with the current system or work within the conventional policy mindset. Yet it should be obvious by this point that tinkering would make no difference worth bothering with.

It should be equally obvious that it is this very mindset – the Keynesian big-government mindset with its addiction to soft money, unsound finance and the short term – which is the root of the problems we are trying to address. It is exactly this mindset which has brought the patient, the European economy and many of our political and social institutions, to the brink of collapse. More of the same would merely push the patient over the edge.

Forget the tinkerers and the Keynesian economists: sound money and sound finance have served us well in the past and would doubtless do so again if we gave them a chance. In any case – like it or not – if we want a safe and sound system then there isn't any alternative. It is worth bearing in mind, of course, that those who originally developed the euro were themselves idealistic: ideals can be realised. The failure of the ideal of the euro, which is a form of multi-state monopoly currency, is exactly

the door to the growth of big government. It follows, then, that the abolition of progressive taxation would create political pressures to rein the size of government back in.

the right opportunity to pursue the development of a monetary system based on ideals that have historically worked in practice.

References

Armitstead, L. (2011), 'Royal Bank of Scotland told by MPs to explain £25bn accounting "distortion"', *Daily Telegraph*, 2 June.

Campbell, D. and N. Griffin (2006), 'Enron and the end of corporate governance', in S. MacLeod (ed.), *Global Governance and the Quest for Justice*, Oxford: Hart Publishing, pp. 47–62.

Carswell, D. (2012), *The End of Politics and the Birth of iDemocracy*, London: Biteback.

Dowd, K. (1988), *Private Money: The Path to Monetary Stability*, Hobart Paper 112, London: Institute of Economic Affairs.

Dowd, K. (ed.) (1992), *The Experience of Free Banking*, London: Routledge.

Dowd, K. (1996), *Competition and Finance: A Reinterpretation of Financial and Monetary Economics*, Basingstoke: Macmillan.

Dowd, K. (1998), 'The misguided drive toward European Monetary Union', in K. Dowd and R. H. Timberlake, Jr (eds), *Money and the Nation State: The Financial Revolution, Government and the World Monetary System*, New Brunswick, NJ: Transaction Publishers/ Oakland, CA: Independent Institute, pp. 351–76.

Dowd, K. (1999), 'An almost ideal monetary rule', *Greek Economic Review*, 19(2): 53–62.

Dowd, K. and M. Hutchinson (2010), *Alchemists of Loss: How Modern Finance and Government Intervention Crashed the Financial System*, Chichester: Wiley.

Dowd, K., M. Hutchinson, S. Ashby and J. Hinchliffe (2011), 'Capital inadequacies: the dismal failure of the Basel system of bank capital regulation', Cato Institute Policy Analysis no. 681, 29 July.

Fisher, I. (1913), 'A compensated dollar', *Quarterly Journal of Economics*, 27: 213–35.

Friedman, M. (1951), 'Commodity-reserve currency', *Journal of Political Economy*, 59(3): 202–32.

Friedman, M. (1968), *Dollars and Deficits: Living with America's Economic Problems*, Englewood Cliffs, NJ: Prentice-Hall.

Horwitz, S. (1992), *Monetary Evolution, Free Banking, and Economic Order*, Boulder, CO: Westview Press.

Jastram, R. W. (2009), *The Golden Constant: The English and American Experience 1560–2007*, Cheltenham: Edward Elgar.

Kerr, G. (2011), *The Law of Opposites: Illusory Profits in the Financial Sector*, London: Adam Smith Institute.

Marshall, A. (1887), 'Remedies for fluctuations of general prices', reprinted in A. C. Pigou (ed.), *Memorials of Alfred Marshall*, New York: Augustus M. Kelley, pp. 188–211.

Schuler, K. (1992a), 'The world history of free banking' in K. Dowd (ed.), *The Experience of Free Banking*, London: Routledge, pp. 7–47.

Schuler, K. (1992b), 'Free banking in Canada', in K. Dowd (ed.), *The Experience of Free Banking*, London: Routledge, pp. 79–92.

Selgin, G. A. (1988), *The Theory of Free Banking: Money Supply under Competitive Note Issue*, Totowa, NJ: Rowman and Littlefield.

Smith, V. (1936), *The Rationale of Central Banking*, London: P. S. King.

White, L. H. (1984), *Free Banking in Britain: Theory, Experience and Debate, 1800–1845*, Cambridge: Cambridge University Press.

Williams, A. (1892), 'A fixed "value of bullion" standard – a proposal for preventing general fluctuations of trade', *Economic Journal*, 2: 280–89.

ABOUT THE IEA

The Institute is a research and educational charity (No. CC 235 351), limited by guarantee. Its mission is to improve understanding of the fundamental institutions of a free society by analysing and expounding the role of markets in solving economic and social problems.

The IEA achieves its mission by:

- a high-quality publishing programme
- conferences, seminars, lectures and other events
- outreach to school and college students
- brokering media introductions and appearances

The IEA, which was established in 1955 by the late Sir Antony Fisher, is an educational charity, not a political organisation. It is independent of any political party or group and does not carry on activities intended to affect support for any political party or candidate in any election or referendum, or at any other time. It is financed by sales of publications, conference fees and voluntary donations.

In addition to its main series of publications the IEA also publishes a termly journal, *Economic Affairs*.

The IEA is aided in its work by a distinguished international Academic Advisory Council and an eminent panel of Honorary Fellows. Together with other academics, they review prospective IEA publications, their comments being passed on anonymously to authors. All IEA papers are therefore subject to the same rigorous independent refereeing process as used by leading academic journals.

IEA publications enjoy widespread classroom use and course adoptions in schools and universities. They are also sold throughout the world and often translated/reprinted.

Since 1974 the IEA has helped to create a worldwide network of 100 similar institutions in over 70 countries. They are all independent but share the IEA's mission.

Views expressed in the IEA's publications are those of the authors, not those of the Institute (which has no corporate view), its Managing Trustees, Academic Advisory Council members or senior staff.

Members of the Institute's Academic Advisory Council, Honorary Fellows, Trustees and Staff are listed on the following page.

The Institute gratefully acknowledges financial support for its publications programme and other work from a generous benefaction by the late Alec and Beryl Warren.

The Institute of Economic Affairs
2 Lord North Street, Westminster, London SW1P 3LB
Tel: 020 7799 8900
Fax: 020 7799 2137
Email: iea@iea.org.uk
Internet: iea.org.uk

Other papers recently published by the IEA include:

Taxation and Red Tape
The Cost to British Business of Complying with the UK Tax System
Francis Chittenden, Hilary Foster & Brian Sloan
Research Monograph 64; ISBN 978 0 255 36612 0; £12.50

Ludwig von Mises – A Primer
Eamonn Butler
Occasional Paper 143; ISBN 978 0 255 36629 8; £7.50

Does Britain Need a Financial Regulator?
Statutory Regulation, Private Regulation and Financial Markets
Terry Arthur & Philip Booth
Hobart Paper 169; ISBN 978 0 255 36593 2; £12.50

Hayek's *The Constitution of Liberty*
An Account of Its Argument
Eugene F. Miller
Occasional Paper 144; ISBN 978 0 255 36637 3; £12.50

Fair Trade Without the Froth
A Dispassionate Economic Analysis of 'Fair Trade'
Sushil Mohan
Hobart Paper 170; ISBN 978 0 255 36645 8; £10.00

A New Understanding of Poverty
Poverty Measurement and Policy Implications
Kristian Niemietz
Research Monograph 65; ISBN 978 0 255 36638 0; £12.50

The Challenge of Immigration
A Radical Solution
Gary S. Becker
Occasional Paper 145; ISBN 978 0 255 36613 7; £7.50

Sharper Axes, Lower Taxes
Big Steps to a Smaller State
Edited by Philip Booth
Hobart Paperback 38; ISBN 978 0 255 36648 9; £12.50

Self-employment, Small Firms and Enterprise
Peter Urwin
Research Monograph 66; ISBN 978 0 255 36610 6; £12.50

Crises of Governments
The Ongoing Global Financial Crisis and Recession
Robert Barro
Occasional Paper 146; ISBN 978 0 255 36657 1; £7.50

... and the Pursuit of Happiness
Wellbeing and the Role of Government
Edited by Philip Booth
Readings 64; ISBN 978 0 255 36656 4; £12.50

Public Choice – A Primer
Eamonn Butler
Occasional Paper 147; ISBN 978 0 255 36650 2; £10.00

The Profit Motive in Education: Continuing the Revolution
Edited by James B. Stanfield
Readings 65; ISBN 978 0 255 36646 5; £12.50

Which Road Ahead – Government or Market?
Oliver Knipping & Richard Wellings
Hobart Paper 171; ISBN 978 0 255 36619 9; £10.00

The Future of the Commons
Beyond Market Failure and Government Regulation
Elinor Ostrom et al.
Occasional Paper 148; ISBN 978 0 255 36653 3; £10.00

Redefining the Poverty Debate
Why a War on Markets is No Substitute for a War on Poverty
Kristian Niemietz
Research Monograph 67; ISBN 978 0 255 36652 6; £12.50

Other IEA publications

Comprehensive information on other publications and the wider work of the IEA can be found at www.iea.org.uk. To order any publication please see below.

Personal customers

Orders from personal customers should be directed to the IEA:
Clare Rusbridge
IEA
2 Lord North Street
FREEPOST LON10168
London SW1P 3YZ
Tel: 020 7799 8907. Fax: 020 7799 2137
Email: crusbridge@iea.org.uk

Trade customers

All orders from the book trade should be directed to the IEA's distributor:
Gazelle Book Services Ltd (IEA Orders)
FREEPOST RLYS-EAHU-YSCZ
White Cross Mills
Hightown
Lancaster LA1 4XS
Tel: 01524 68765. Fax: 01524 53232
Email: sales@gazellebooks.co.uk

IEA subscriptions

The IEA also offers a subscription service to its publications. For a single annual payment (currently £42.00 in the UK), subscribers receive every monograph the IEA publishes. For more information please contact:
Clare Rusbridge
Subscriptions
IEA
2 Lord North Street
FREEPOST LON10168
London SW1P 3YZ
Tel: 020 7799 8907. Fax: 020 7799 2137
Email: crusbridge@iea.org.uk